THE DEEPER
CHRISTIAN LIFE

THE DEEPER CHRISTIAN LIFE

ANDREW MURRAY

FRANCIS ASBURY PRESS
of Zondervan Publishing House

Grand Rapids, Michigan

THE DEEPER CHRISTIAN LIFE

Copyright © 1985 by
The Zondervan Corporation
Grand Rapids, Michigan

FRANCIS ASBURY PRESS
is an imprint of
Zondervan Publishing House
1415 Lake Drive S.E.
Grand Rapids, Michigan 49506

Library of Congress Cataloging in Publication Data

Murray, Andrew, 1828–1917.
    The deeper Christian life.
      1. Spiritual life—Reformed authors.   2. Holiness.
    I. Title.

BV4501.M7972   1985   248.4'842   85–20292

ISBN   0–310–29791–5

Edited by Lyman Rand Tucker, Jr.

Designed by Louise Bauer

Printed in the United States of America

85 86 87 88 89 90 / 10 9 8 7 6 5 4 3 2 1

CONTENTS

FOREWORD:
ANDREW MURRAY'S MODERN SIGNIFICANCE

Andrew Murray, known to the Christian world today primarily for his books on prayer, was a leading figure in the Holiness Movement in the latter half of the last century.

That may come as a surprise to many readers who are familiar with some of his writings. Two factors are involved here. First, his denominational and theological associations seem inappropriate. He was a member of the Dutch Reformed Church and was educated in Scotland (Aberdeen) and Holland (Utrecht). He served throughout a long life as a pastor and leader in a church noted for its roots in high Calvinism. Today we do not expect a person from that segment of the body of Christ and from that theological tradition to be identified as a foremost spokesman for the Holiness Movement.

A second factor that may explain this surprise is that the Holiness Movement today is much less inclusive than it was in the nineteenth century. Its leaders at that time—whose present-day descendants would tend to disavow any connection with the holiness message— were tagged by their contemporaries as holiness preachers, and they freely and humbly welcomed that tag.

It was a time of revival. In the United States the Spirit's movement that had been seen in frontier camp meetings reached into the urban scene. Great cities felt the impact of the gospel in revival power. As the Spirit crossed sociological lines, He also transcended the bounds of our theological and ecclesiological divisions.

The hunger for God was so great that normal divisions were forgotten. The cries of the unregenerate worldling and the nominal churchman for reconciliation with God were matched or exceeded by those of believers seeking a deeper experience of God's grace. New School Presbyterians joined Oberlin perfectionists and Arminian Methodists in the insistence that justification was not enough. Carnal believers must have a deeper work of God's Spirit in them if the work of God were to be done. So, together they sought personal holiness.

That hunger was not confined to America. The emergence of Keswick in England was a sign and a focal point in Britain. Europe and many mission fields felt the touch of God. South Africa, where Murray labored, was not exempted. God moved, and where He moved, the body of believers sought Pentecostal empowerment and blessing.

Perhaps the key to Murray's life was the hunger for revival. Some of this came from his father. It was Andrew Murray, Sr.'s custom to shut himself in his study every Friday evening. He would read the accounts of revivals in Scotland and elsewhere in the past as well as any records of outpourings of the Spirit in his own time. Then he would pray for a similar movement of the Spirit upon his own church and world. The younger Murray recalled how he would stand outside the study door listening to his father crying out to God for revival.

Years later (in 1860, when the younger Andrew was thirty-two) Andrew, Sr. was in a conference where he heard of the revival fires that were sweeping America, Ireland, Scotland, England, and his own South Africa. He publicly broke into tears as he openly rejoiced and spoke of how his heart had yearned for just that. The hunger for God that marked the father was to mark the son as well.

That concern for revival caused Murray to see that many Christians were living below their privilege as believers. He also knew that no great blessing could come through or to Christians who were less than wholehearted. The yearning of his heart for God's blessing opened him to possibilities in grace that had not been emphasized in his tradition. One of these was the possibility of a life wholly surrendered to God and lived in unbroken communion with God, a life characterized by the Spirit's anointing and empowerment. Another was the privilege of divine healing for the believer. The former of these is our concern here.

The result of his concern was that he began to differentiate between two levels of Christian living. One was that of the typical believer who knew the regenerating power of Christ but who had not come to a place of absolute and complete surrender to Him. So he wrote (in *The Two Covenants* [Fort Washington, Pa.: Christian Literature Crusade, n.d.], p. 17):

> . . . everywhere throughout the Church, there are to be found two classes of Christians. Some are content with the mingled life, half flesh and half spirit, half self effort and half grace. Others are not content with this, but are seeking with their whole heart to know to the full what the deliverance from sin and what the abiding full power for a walk in God's presence is, which the New Covenant has brought and can give. God help us to be satisfied with nothing less.

The difference between the two kinds of Christians became sharper for Andrew Murray. His burden increased to see more and more believers move to the higher level.

This burden began to reflect itself in his thinking, his preaching, and his writing. He began to use the language of absolute surrender, the fullness of the Spirit, the baptism of the Spirit, the second blessing, perfection, holiness, and the life of unbroken victory. Note the titles of some of his books (e.g., *Abide in Christ, Absolute Surrender, Be Perfect, Freedom from a Self-Centered Life, The Full Blessing of Christ, The Holiest of All, The Power of the Spirit, The Spiritual Life, The Two Covenants, and Wholly for God*). A look at these indicates where his burden was.

It is little wonder that Murray came under attack from some of his colleagues. There seems to have been some suspicion that he was not firm enough in his Calvinism. His biographer, Leona Choy, tells us that in 1868, when he was in his prime—pastor of the Dutch Reformed Church in Capetown and moderator of his denomination—it became necessary for him to defend himself in the public press against the charge of false teaching. The accusations were that he taught that people are lost or saved through their own free will, that human beings can frustrate God's will to redeem them, and that God wills the redemption of all. Apparently Murray defended himself successfully against these charges of heresy. The controversy did not deter him, though, in his concern to seek revival and to preach holiness, even if at times it made him sound somewhat like a Wesleyan.

What was Murray's ultimate theological stance? Was he really more Calvinistic than Wesleyan, if one must use these terms of him? One gets the feeling from reading Murray that such classifications were no great concern of his. The reader does not have to go far in Murray before becoming aware that Murray's passion was not as much that of fidelity to a classical theological position as it was that of fidelity to the Word and to the God who inspired it and of whom it speaks. His concern was to be biblical and to bring his readers to the highest level of grace available through Christ's passion and the Spirit's coming.

Quotations from the classical theologians or references to the Fathers are not prominent in Murray; his emphasis is on confrontation with the Word and with the Lord who is the Word. The result was that he ultimately satisfied neither the Calvinists nor the Wesleyans completely. That he was an instrument of the Spirit for the promotion of the message and experience of holiness is without question. So, he tagged himself, just as his contemporaries tagged him, as a holiness preacher.

Note his words to students at Moody Bible Institute in 1895. He was dealing with the reality of spiritual defeat in many believers' lives. He spoke of those who had, without success, fought for years to master temper, self-will, or an unloving spirit. Then he said (in *The Spiritual Life* [Philadelphia: George W. Jacobs, 1897], p. 183):

> Oh, the blessedness of knowing there is a second step! That second step need not be long after conversion, when the Holy Spirit comes very mightily down upon a man and he at once begins to will and to do. But in the Church as it is now, in most cases it does not come at once, and therefore we must preach to you, beloved brethren, that there is a different stage from that, on

which most of us live. And what is that stage? That stage is when the Holy Spirit comes and fills the heart and a man believes, not only God does work in me *to will*, but God will work in me *to do*. Oh, the difference between willing and doing.

For Murray, that second step can be as clear and as marked—as wonderful—as conversion.

Occasionally some wonder at the value of reprints. Why reprint now a work that is almost a century old? The reality is that the human problem never really changes. Self-sufficiency, self-will, and self-satisfaction in Christians hinder the purposes of God now as much as they ever did. The insights of Murray as he deals with sin in believers and with the possibilities in grace are thus as relevant now as when he wrote them.

When Murray spoke and wrote, God blessed. The Spirit found his words good vehicles for His own purposes. Sin and carnal self-interest were laid bare. The Spirit was able to bring readers to consciousness of need, repentance, surrender, and faith. The results were transformation for many. Victory came where there had been defeat, heart cleansing where there had been defiling self-interest. That is the burden behind the Francis Asbury imprint series. So, we present Andrew Murray to help hungry readers like ourselves find the deliverance that will enable us to "serve him without fear, in holiness and righteousness . . . all the days of our life" (Luke 1:74–75).

What a glorious thing if God would in the end of this century do a work like that He did in the end of the last century. Murray was an instrument then. May he be again!

Dennis F. Kinlaw
Francis Asbury Society
Wilmore, Kentucky

DAILY FELLOWSHIP WITH GOD

DAILY FELLOWSHIP
WITH GOD

HE first and chief need of our Christian life is *fellowship with God.*

The divine life within us comes from God and is entirely dependent upon Him. As I need every moment afresh the air to breathe, as the sun every moment afresh sends down its light, so it is only in direct living communication with God that my soul can be strong.

The manna of one day was corrupt when the next day came. I must every day have fresh grace from heaven, and I obtain it only in direct waiting upon God Himself. Begin each day by tarrying before God and letting Him touch you. Take time to meet God.

To this end, let your first act in your devotions be setting yourself still before God. In prayer, or worship, everything depends upon God taking the chief place. I must bow quietly before Him in humble faith and adoration, speaking thus within my heart: "God is. God is near. God is love, longing to communicate

Himself to me. God the Almighty One, Who worketh all in all, is even now waiting to work in me and make Himself known." *Take time, till you know God is very near.*

When you have given God His place of honor, glory, and power, take your place of deepest lowliness, and seek to be filled with the Spirit of humility. As a creature, it is your blessedness to be nothing, that God may be all in you. As a sinner, you are not worthy to look up to God; bow in self-abasement. As a saint, let God's love overwhelm you and bow you still lower down. Sink down before Him in humility, meekness, patience, and surrender to His goodness and mercy. He will exalt you. *Oh! take time to get very low before God.*

Then accept and value your place in Christ Jesus. God delights in nothing but His beloved Son; He can be satisfied with nothing else in those who draw nigh to Him. Enter deep into God's holy presence in the boldness which the blood gives and in the assurance that in Christ you are most well-pleasing. In Christ you are within the veil. You have access into the very heart and love of the Father. This is the great object of fellowship with God: that I may have more of God in my life and that God may see Christ formed in me. Be silent before God and let Him bless you.

This Christ is a living Person. He loves you with a personal love, and He looks every day for the personal response of your love. Look into His face with trust, till His love really shines into your heart. Make His heart glad by telling Him that you do love Him. He offers Himself to you as a personal Savior and Keeper from the power of sin. Do not ask, can I be kept from sinning, if I keep close to Him? but ask, can I be kept from sinning, *if He always keeps close to me?* and you see at once how safe it is to trust Him.

We have not only Christ's life in us as a power and His presence with us as a person; we have His likeness to be wrought into us. He is to be formed in us, so that His form or figure, His likeness, can be seen in us. Bow before God until you get some sense of the greatness and blessedness of the work to be carried on by God in you this day. Say to God, "Father, here am I for Thee to give as much in me of Christ's likeness as I can receive." And wait to hear Him say, "My child, I give thee as much of Christ as thy heart is open to receive." The God who revealed Jesus in the flesh and perfected Him will reveal Him in thee and perfect thee in Him. The Father loves the Son and delights to work out His image and likeness in thee. Count upon it that this blessed work will be done in thee as thou waitest on thy God and holdest fellowship with Him.

The likeness to Christ consists chiefly in two things—the likeness of His death and the likeness of His resurrection (Rom. 6:5). The death of Christ was the consummation of His humility and obedience, the entire giving up of His life to God. In Him we are dead to sin. As we sink down in humility and dependence and entire surrender to God, the power of His death works in us, and we are made conformable to His death. And so we know Him in the power of His resurrection, in the victory over sin, and in all the joy and power of the risen life. Therefore, every morning, present yourselves unto God "as those that are alive from the dead." He will maintain the life He gave; He will bestow the grace to live as risen ones.

All this can come about only in the power of the Holy Spirit, who dwells in you. Count upon Him to glorify Christ in you. Count upon Christ to increase in you the inflowing of His Spirit. As you wait before

God to realize His presence, remember that the Spirit is in you to reveal the things of God. Seek in God's presence to have the anointing of the Spirit of Christ so truly that your whole life may every moment be spiritual.

As you meditate on this wondrous salvation, seek full fellowship with the great and holy God, and wait on Him to reveal Christ in you, you will feel how needful it is to give up all to receive Him. Seek grace to know what it means to live as wholly for God as Christ did. Only the Holy Spirit Himself can teach you what an entire yielding of the whole life to God can mean. Wait on God to show you in this what you do not know. Let every approach to God and every request for fellowship with Him be accompanied by a new, very definite, and entire surrender to Him to work in you.

"By faith" must here, as through all Scripture and all the spiritual life, be the keynote. As you tarry before God, let it be in a deep, quiet faith in Him, the Invisible One, who is so near, so holy, so mighty, so loving. In a deep, restful faith, too, that all the blessings and powers of the heavenly life are around you, and in you. Just yield yourself in the faith of a perfect trust to the Ever Blessed Holy Trinity to work out all God's purpose in you. Begin each day thus in fellowship with God, and God will be all in all to you.

PRIVILEGE AND EXPERIENCE

PRIVILEGE AND EXPERIENCE

And he said unto him, Son, thou art ever with me, and all that I have is thine (Luke 15:31).

HE words of the text are familiar to us all. The elder son had complained that though his father had made a feast and had killed the fatted calf for the prodigal son, he had never given him even a kid that he might make merry with his friends. The answer of the father was: "Son, thou art ever with me, and all that I have is thine." One cannot have a more wonderful revelation of the heart of our Father in heaven than this. We often speak of the wonderful revelation of the father's heart in his welcome to the prodigal son and in what he did for him. But here, in what he says to the elder son, we have a far more wonderful revelation of the father's love.

If we are to experience a deepening of spiritual life, we want, on the one hand, to discover clearly what is the spiritual life that God would have us live and, on the other, to ask whether we are living that life or, if not, what hinders us living it out fully.

This subject naturally divides itself into four heads: (1) the high privilege of every child of God, (2) the low experience of too many of us believers, (3) the cause of the discrepancy between God's gifts and our low experience, and (4) the way to the restoration of the privilege.

THE HIGH PRIVILEGE
OF THE CHILDREN OF GOD

We have here two things describing the privilege: first, "Son, thou art ever with me" (unbroken fellowship with thy Father is thy portion) and second, "All that I have is thine" (all that God can bestow upon His children is theirs).

"Thou art ever with me." I am always near thee; thou canst dwell every hour of thy life in My presence, and all I have is for thee. I am a father, with a loving father's heart. I will withhold no good thing from thee. In these promises, we have the rich privileges of God's heritage. We have, in the first place, unbroken fellowship with Him. A father never sends his child away with the thought that he does not care about his child knowing that he loves him. The father longs to have his child believe that he has the light of his father's countenance upon him all the day—that, if he sends the child away to school, or anywhere that necessity compels, it is with a sense of sacrifice of parental feelings. If it be so with an earthly father, what think you of God? Does He not want every child of His to know that he is constantly living in the light of His countenance? This is the meaning of that word, "Son, thou art ever with me."

That was the privilege of God's people in Old Testament times. We are told that "Enoch walked with God." God's promise to Jacob was: "Behold, I am with thee, and will keep thee in all places whither thou goest, and will bring thee again into this land; for I will not leave thee until I have done that which I have spoken to thee of." And God's promise to Israel through Moses was: "My presence shall go with thee, and I will give thee rest." And in Moses' response to the promise, he says, "For wherein shall it be known that I and Thy people have found grace in Thy sight? It is not that Thou goest with us; so shall we be separated, I and Thy people, from all the people that are upon the face of the earth." The presence of God with Israel was the mark of their separation from other people. This is the truth taught in all the Old Testament; and if so, how much more may we look for it in the New Testament? Thus, we find our Savior promising to those who love Him and who keep His word, that the Father also will love them, and Father and Son will come and make Their abode with them.

Let that thought into your hearts—that the child of God is called to this blessed privilege, to live every moment in fellowship with God. Each believer is called to enjoy the full light of His countenance. There are many Christians—I suppose the majority of Christians—who seem to regard the whole of the Spirit's work as confined to conviction and conversion, not that He came to dwell in our hearts and there reveal God to us. He came not to dwell near us but in us, that we might be *filled* with His indwelling. We are commanded to be "*filled* with the Spirit"; then the Holy Spirit would make God's presence manifest to us. That is the whole teaching of the Epistle to the Hebrews: the veil is rent in twain; we have access into the holiest of all by the blood of Jesus; we come into the very presence of God, so that we can live all the day with that presence resting upon us. That presence is with us wheresoever we go; and in all kinds of trouble, we have undisturbed repose and peace. "Son, thou art ever with me."

There are some people who seem to think that God, by some unintelligible sovereignty, withdraws His face. But I know that God loves His people too much to withhold His fellowship from them for any such reason. The true reason of the absence of God from us is rather to be found in our sin and unbelief than in any supposed sovereignty of His. If the child of God is walking in faith and obedience, the divine presence will be enjoyed in unbroken continuity.

Then there is the next blessed privilege: *"All that I have is thine."* Thank God, He has given us His own Son; and in giving Him, He has given us all things that are in Him—Christ's life, His love, His Spirit, His glory. "All are yours, and ye are Christ's, and Christ is God's." All the riches of His Son, the everlasting King, God bestows upon every one of His children. "Son, thou art ever with me; and all that I have is thine." Is not that the meaning of all those wonderful promises given in connection with prayer: "Whatsoever ye shall ask in My name, ye shall receive"? Yes, there it is. That is the life of the children of God, as He Himself has pictured it to us.

In contrast with this high privilege of believers, look at the low experience of many believers.

THE LOW EXPERIENCE OF TOO MANY OF US

The elder son was living with his father and serving him "these many years," and he complains that his father never gave him a kid but did give his prodigal brother the fatted calf. Why was this? Simply because the elder son did not ask for it. He did not believe that he would get it, and therefore never asked it and never enjoyed it. He continued thus to live in constant murmuring and dissatisfaction; and the keynote of all this wretched life is furnished in what he said. His father gave him everything, yet he never enjoyed it; and he throws the whole blame on his loving and kind father. O beloved, is not that the life of many a believer? Do not many speak and act in this way? Every believer has the promise of unbroken fellowship with God, but he says, "I have not enjoyed it; I have tried hard and done my best, and I have prayed for the blessing, but I suppose God does not see fit to grant it." But why not? One says, it is the sovereignty of God withholding the blessing. The father withheld not his gifts from the elder brother in sovereignty; neither does our Heavenly Father withhold any good thing from them that love Him. He does not make any such differences between His children. "He is able to make all grace abound towards you" was a promise equally made to all in the Corinthian church.

Some think these rich blessings are not for them; they are for those who have more time to devote to religion and prayer. Or, they say, their circumstances are so difficult, so peculiar, that we can have no conception of their various hindrances. But do not such think that God, if He places them in these circumstances, cannot make His grace abound accordingly? They admit He could if He would, work a miracle for them, which they can hardly expect. In some way, they, like the elder son, throw the blame on God. Thus, many are saying, when asked if they are enjoying unbroken fellowship with God: "Alas, no! I have not been able to attain to such a height; it is too high for me. I know of some who have it, and I read of it; but God has not given it to me, for some reason." But why not? You think, perhaps, that you have not the same capacity for spiritual blessing that others have. The Bible speaks of a joy that is "unspeakable and full of glory" as the fruit of believing; of a "love of God shed abroad in our hearts by the Holy Ghost." Do we enjoy these blessings? If not, why? We desire it, or do we? Why not get it? Have we asked for it? We think we are not worthy of the blessing, not good enough, and therefore God has not given it. There are more among us than we know of, or are willing to admit, who throw the blame of our darkness and of our wanderings on God! Take care! Take care! Take care!

And again, what about that other promise? The Father says, "All I have is thine." Are you rejoicing in the treasures of Christ? Are you conscious of having an abundant supply for all your spiritual needs every day? God has all these for you in abundance. "Thou never gavest me a kid!" The answer is, "All that I have is thine. I gave it thee in Christ."

Dear reader, we have such wrong thoughts of God. What is God like? I know no image more beautiful and instructive than that of the sun. The sun is never weary of shining, of pouring out his beneficent rays upon both the good and the evil. Although you might close up the windows with blinds or bricks, the sun would shine upon them all the same; though we might sit in darkness, in utter darkness, the shining would be just the same. God's sun shines on every leaf, on every flower, on every blade of grass, on everything that springs out of the ground. All receive this wealth of sunshine until they grow to perfection and bear fruit. Would He who made that sun be less willing to pour out His love and life into me? The sun—what beauty it creates! And my God, would He not delight more in creating a beauty and a fruitfulness in me—such, too, as He has *promised* to give? And yet some say, when asked why they do not live in unbroken communion with God, "God does not give it to me, I do not know why; but that is the only reason I can give you—He has not given it to me." You remember the parable of the one who said, "I know thou art an hard master, reaping where thou hast not sown and gathering where thou has not strawed" (asking and demanding what thou hast not given). Oh! let us come and ask why it is that the believer lives such a low experience.

THE CAUSE OF THIS DISCREPANCY BETWEEN GOD'S GIFTS AND OUR LOW EXPERIENCE

The believer is complaining that God has never given him a kid. Or, God has given him some blessing but has never given the full blessing. He has never filled him with His Spirit. "I never," he says, "had my heart, as a fountain, giving forth the rivers of living waters promised in John 7:38." What is the cause? The elder son thought he was serving his father faithfully "these many years" in his father's house, but it was in the spirit of bondage and not in the spirit of a child, so that his unbelief blinded him to the conception of a father's love and kindness, and he was unable all the time to see that his father was ready to give him, not only a kid, but a hundred, or a thousand, kids, if he would have them. He was simply living in unbelief, in ignorance, in blindness, robbing himself of the privileges that the father had for him. So, if there be a discrepancy between our life and the fulfillment and enjoyment of all God's promises, the fault is ours. If our experience be not what God wants it to be, it is because of our unbelief in the love of God, in the power of God, and in the reality of God's promises.

God's Word teaches us, in the story of the Israelites, that the cause of their troubles was unbelief on their part, not any limitation or restriction on God's part. As Psalm 78 says: "He clave the rocks in the wilderness, and gave them drink as out of the great depths. He brought streams also out of the rock, and caused waters to run down like rivers" (vv. 15–16). Yet they sinned by doubting His power to provide meat for them. "They spake against God; they said, Can God furnish a table in the wilderness?" (v. 19). Later on we read, "They turned back and tempted God, and limited the Holy One of Israel" (v. 41). They kept distrusting Him from time to time. When they got to Kadesh-Barnea, and God told them to enter the land flowing with milk and honey—where would be rest, abundance, and victory—only two men (Caleb and Joshua) said, "The LORD is with us: fear them not." But the ten spies had said, "We be not able to go up against the people; for they are stronger than we," and this majority opinion prevailed. It was simply unbelief that kept them out of the Land of Promise.

If there is to be any deepening of the spiritual life in

us, we must come to the discovery and the acknowl-edgment of the unbelief there is in our hearts. God grant that we may get this spiritual quickening, and that we may come to see that it is by our own unbelief that we have prevented God from doing His work in us. Unbelief is the mother of disobedience, and of all my sins and shortcomings—my temper, my pride, my unlovingness, my worldliness, my sins of every kind. Though these differ in nature and form, yet they all come from the one root, viz., that we do not believe in the freedom and fullness of the divine gift of the Holy Spirit to dwell in us and strengthen us and fill us with the life and grace of God all the day long. Look, I pray you, at that elder son, and ask what was the cause of that terrible difference between the heart of the father and the experience of the son. There can be no answer but that it was this sinful unbelief that utterly blinded the son to a sense of his father's love.

Dear fellow-believer, I want to say to you, that, if you are not living in the joy of God's salvation, the entire cause is your unbelief. You do not believe in the mighty power of God and His willingness, by His Holy Spirit, to work a thorough change in your life and enable you to live in fullness of consecration to Him. God is willing that you should so live; but you do not believe it.

If human beings really believed in the infinite love of God, what a change it would bring about! What is love? It is a desire to communicate oneself for the good of the object loved—the opposite of selfishness; as we read in 1 Corinthians 13:5, love "seeketh not her own." Thus, the mother is willing to sacrifice herself for the good of her child. So God in His love is ever willing to impart blessing; and He is omnipotent in His love. This is true, my friends; God is *omnipotent* in love, and He is doing His utmost to fill every heart in this house. "But if God is really anxious to do that, and if He is Almighty, why does He not do it now?" You must remember that God has given you a will, and by the exercise of that will you can hinder God and remain content, like the elder son, with the low life of unbelief. Come, now, and let us see that the cause of the difference between God's high, blessed provision for His children, and the low, sad experience of many of us lies in the unbelief that distrusts and grieves Him.

THE WAY OF RESTORATION: HOW IS THAT TO BE BROUGHT ABOUT?

We all know not only the parable of the prodigal son but also how many sermons about repentance have been preached from that parable. We are told that "when he came to himself he said, . . . I will arise and go to my father, and will say unto him, Father, I have sinned against heaven, and in thy sight." In preaching, we speak of this as the first step in a changed life—as conversion, repentance, confession, returning to God. But, as this is the first step for the prodigal, we must remember that this is also the step to be taken by God's erring children—by all the ninety-nine "who need no repentance," or think they do not. Those Christians who do not understand how wrong their low religious life is must be taught that it is sin—unbelief—and that it is as necessary for them as for the prodigal to be brought to repentance. You have heard a great deal of preaching repentance to the unconverted; but I want to try to preach it to God's children. That elder brother pictures so many of God's children. What the father told him—to bring about a consideration of the love that he bore him, just as he loved the prodigal brother—thus does God tell to us in our contentedness with such a low life: "You must repent and believe that I love you, and all that I have is thine." He says, "By your unbelief, you have dishonored Me, living for ten, twenty, or thirty years and never believing what it was to live in the blessedness of My love. You must confess the wrong you have done Me in this, and be broken down in contrition of heart just as truly as the prodigal."

There are many children of God who need to confess that though they are His children, they have never believed that God's promises are true, that He is willing to fill their hearts all the day long with His blessed presence. Have *you* believed this? If you have not, all our teaching will be of no profit to you. Will you not say, "By the help of God, I will begin now a life of faith and will not rest until I know what such a life means. I will believe that I am every moment in the Father's presence and that all that He has is mine"?

May the Lord God work this conviction in the hearts of all cold believers. Have you ever heard the expression, "a conviction for sanctification?" You know, the unconverted person needs conviction before conversion. So does the dark-minded Christian need conviction before (and in order to obtain) sanctification and before he comes to a real insight to spiritual blessedness. He must be convicted a second time because of his sinful life of doubt and temper and unlovingness. He must be broken down under that conviction; then there is hope for him. May the Father of mercy grant all such that deep contrition, so that they may be led into the blessedness of His presence, and enjoy the fulness of His power and love!

CARNAL
OR SPIRITUAL?

CARNAL OR
SPIRITUAL?

And Peter went out and wept bitterly (Luke 22:62).

HESE words indicate the turning point in the life of Peter—a crisis. There is often a question about the life of holiness. Do you grow into it? or do you come into it by a crisis suddenly? Peter had been growing for three years under the training of Christ, but he had grown terribly downward; for at the end of his growing he denied Jesus. And then there came a crisis. After the crisis he was a changed man, and then he began to grow aright. We must indeed grow in grace, but before we can grow in grace we must be put right.

You know what the two halves of the life of Peter were. In God's Word we read very often about the difference between the carnal and the spiritual Christian. The word "carnal" comes from the Latin word for flesh. In Romans 8 and in Galatians 5, we are taught that the flesh and the Spirit of God are the two opposing powers by which we are dominated or ruled, and we are taught that a true believer may allow himself to be ruled by the flesh. That is what Paul writes to the Corinthians. In the first four verses of the third chapter, he says four times to them, "You are carnal, not spiritual." And just so a believer can allow the flesh to have so much power over him that he becomes "carnal." Every object is named according to its most prominent characteristic. If a man is a babe in Christ and has a little of the Holy Spirit and a great deal of the flesh, he is called *carnal*, for the flesh is his chief mark. If he gives way, as the Corinthians did, to strife, temper, division, and envy, he is a carnal Christian. He is a Christian, but a carnal one. But if he gives himself over entirely to the Holy Spirit so that He (the Holy Spirit) can deliver from the temper, the envy, and the strife by breathing a heavenly disposition and can mortify the deeds of the body, then God's Word calls him a "spiritual" man, a true spiritual Christian.

Now, these two styles are remarkably illustrated in the life of Peter. The text is the crisis and turning point at which he begins to pass over from the one side to the other.

The message that I want to bring to you is this: That the great majority of Christians, alas, are not spiritual men, and that they may become spiritual men by the grace of God. To all who are perhaps hungering and longing for the better life and asking what is wrong that you are without it, I want to point out that what is wrong is simply this: *allowing the flesh to rule in you and trusting in the power of the flesh to make you good.*

There is a better life, a life in the power of the Holy Spirit.

Then, I want to tell you a third thing. The first

thing is important—take care of the carnal life and confess if you are in it. The second truth is very blessed—there is a spiritual life; believe that it is a possibility. But the third truth is the most important—you can by one step get out of the carnal into the spiritual state. May God reveal it to you now through the story of the apostle Peter!

Look at him, first of all, in the carnal state. What are the marks of the carnal state in him? Self-will, self-pleasing, self-confidence. Just remember, when Christ said to the disciples at Caesarea Philippi, "The Son of Man must be crucified," Peter said to Him, "Lord, that can never be!" And Christ had to say to him, "Get thee behind Me, Satan!" Dear reader, what an awful thing for Peter! He could not understand what a suffering Christ was. And Peter was so self-willed and self-confident that he dared to contradict and to rebuke Christ! Just think of it! Then, you remember how Peter and the other disciples were more than once quarrelling as to who was to be the chief—self-exaltation, self-pleasing—every one wanted the chief seat in the kingdom of God. Then again, remember the last night, when Christ warned Peter that Satan had desired to sift him and that he would deny Him; and Peter said twice over, "Lord, if they all deny Thee, I am ready to go to prison and to death." What self-confidence! He was sure that his heart was right. He loved Jesus, but he trusted himself. "I will never deny my Lord."

Don't you see the whole of that life of Peter is carnal confidence in himself. In his carnal pride, in his carnal unlovingness, in the carnal liberty he took in contradicting Jesus, it was all just the life of the flesh. Peter had loved Jesus. God had by the Holy Spirit taught him. Christ had said, "Flesh and blood hath not revealed it unto thee, but My Father which is in heaven." God had taught him that Christ was the Son of God; but with all that, Peter was only under the power of the flesh; and that is why Christ said at Gethsemane, "The spirit indeed is willing, but the flesh is weak" ("You are under the power of the flesh; you cannot watch with Me."). Dear reader, what did it all lead to? The flesh led not only to the sins I have mentioned but also, last of all, to the saddest of things—Peter's actual denial of Jesus. Three times over he told the lie, once with an oath, "I know not the man." He denied his blessed Lord. That is what it comes to with the life of the flesh. That is Peter.

Now look, in the second place, at Peter after he became a spiritual man. Christ had taught Peter a great deal. I think, if you count carefully, you will find some seven or eight times that Christ had spoken to the disciples about humility. He had taken a little child and set him in the midst of them. He had said three or four times, "He that exalteth himself shall be abased, and he that humbleth himself shall be exalted." He had at the last supper washed their feet. But not even all of this had taught Peter humility. All Christ's instructions were in vain. Remember that now. A man who is not spiritual—though he may read his Bible, though he may listen to the most earnest preaching, though he may study God's Word—cannot conquer sin, because he is not living the life of the Holy Spirit. God has so ordered it, that man cannot live a right Christian life unless he is full of the Holy Ghost. Do you wonder at what I say? Have you been accustomed to think, " 'Full of the Holy Ghost,' that is what the apostles had to be on the day of Pentecost; that is what the martyrs and the ministers had to be; but for *every* man to be full of the Holy Ghost, that is too high"? I tell you solemnly, if you believe that, you will never become thoroughgoing Christians. I must be full of the Holy Spirit if I am to be a wholehearted Christian.

Then, note what change took place in Peter. The Lord Jesus led him up to Pentecost, the Holy Spirit came from heaven upon him, and what took place? The old Peter was gone, and he was a new Peter. Just read his first epistle, and note the keynote of the epistle— "Through suffering to glory." Peter—who had said, "Of course, Lord, you never can suffer or be crucified," who, to save himself suffering or shame, had denied Christ—Peter becomes so changed that when he writes his epistle, the chief thought is the very thought of Christ, "Suffering is the way to glory." Do you not see that the Holy Spirit had changed Peter?

And look at other aspects. Look at Peter. He was so weak that a woman could frighten him into denying Christ; but when the Holy Spirit came he was bold, *bold*, BOLD to confess his Lord at any cost, ready to go to prison and to death for Christ's sake. The Holy Spirit had changed the man. Look at his views of divine truth. He could not understand what Christ taught him; he could not take it in. It was impossible before the death of Christ; but on the day of Pentecost how he is able to expound the Word of God as a spiritual man! I tell you, beloved, when the Holy Ghost comes upon a man, he becomes a spiritual man; and instead of denying his Lord he denies himself, just remember that. In the sixteenth chapter of Matthew, when Peter had said, "Lord, be it far from Thee, this shall never happen that Thou shalt be crucified," Christ said to him: "Peter, not only will I be crucified, but *you* will have to be crucified too. If any man is to be My disciple, let him take up his cross to die upon it, let him deny himself, and let him follow Me." How did Peter obey that command? He went and denied Jesus! As long as a man, a Christian, is under the power of the flesh, he is continually denying Jesus. You always must do one of the two—you must deny self or you must deny Jesus—and, alas, Peter denied his Lord rather than deny himself. On the other hand, when the Holy Spirit came upon him, he could not deny his Lord, but he could deny himself, and he praised God for the privilege of suffering for Christ.

Now, how did the change come about? The words of my text tell us, "And Peter went out and wept bitterly." What does that mean? It means this, that the Lord led Peter to come to the end of himself, to see what was in his heart and with his self-confidence to fall into the very deepest sin that a child of God could be guilty of—publicly, with an oath, to deny his Lord! When Peter stood there in that great sin, the loving Jesus looked upon him; and that look, full of loving reproach, loving pity, pierced like an arrow through the heart of Peter, and he went out and wept bitterly. Praise God, that was the end of self-confident Peter! Praise God, that was the turning point of his life! He went out with a shame that no tongue can express. He woke up as out of a dream to the terrible reality "I have helped to crucify the blessed Son of God." No man can fathom what Peter must have passed through that Friday, Saturday, and Sunday morning. But, blessed be God, on that Sunday Jesus revealed Himself to Peter, we know not how, but "He was seen of Simon." Then in the evening He came to him with the other disciples and breathed peace and the Holy Spirit upon him; and then, later on, you know how three times the Lord

asked him, "Simon, son of Jonas, lovest thou Me?"—
until Peter was sorrowful, and said, "Lord, Thou
knowest all things, Thou knowest that I love Thee."
What was it that wrought the transition from the love
of the flesh to the love of the Spirit? I tell you, the
beginning was when "Peter went out and wept bitterly," with a broken heart, with a heart that would give
anything to show its love to Jesus. With a heart that had
learned to give up all self-confidence, Peter was
prepared for the blessing of the Holy Spirit.

And, now, you can easily see the application of this
story. Are there not many just living the life of Peter, of
the self-confident Peter as he was? Are there not many
who are mourning under the consciousness, "I am so
unfaithful to my Lord. I have no power against the
flesh. I cannot conquer my temper. I give way just like
Peter to the fear of man, of company. For people can
influence me and make me do things I do not want to
do, and I have no power to resist them. Circumstances
get the mastery over me, and I then say and do things
that I am ashamed of"? Is there not more than one,
who, in answer to the question, "Are you living as a
man filled with the Spirit, devoted to Jesus, following
Him, fully giving up all for Him?" must say with
sorrow, "God knows I am not. Alas, my heart knows
it"? You say it, and I come, and I press you with the
question, "Is not your position, and your character, and
your conduct, just like that of Peter?" Like Peter you
love Jesus, like Peter you know He is the Christ of
God, like Peter you are very zealous in working for
Him. Peter had cast out devils in His name, had
preached the gospel, and had healed the sick. Like Peter
you have tried to work for Jesus; but, oh, under it all,
isn't there something that comes up continually? Oh,

Christian, what is it? I pray and I try and I do long to live a holy life, but the flesh is too strong, and sin gets the better of me, and continually I am pleasing self instead of denying it, denying Jesus instead of pleasing Him. Come, all who are willing to make that confession, and let me ask you to look quietly at the other life that is possible for you.

Just as the Lord Jesus gave the Holy Spirit to Peter, He is willing to give the Holy Spirit to you. Are you willing to receive Him? Are you willing to give up yourself entirely as an empty, helpless vessel, to receive the power of the Holy Spirit, to live, to dwell, and to work in you every day? Dear believer, God has prepared such a beautiful and such a blessed life for every one of us, and God as a Father is waiting to see why you will not come to Him and let Him fill you with the Holy Ghost. Are you willing for it? I am sure some are. There are some who have said often, "O God, why can't I live that life? Why can't I live every hour in unbroken fellowship with God? Why can't I enjoy what my Father has given me—all the riches of His grace? It is for me He gave it, and why can't I enjoy it?" There are those who say, "Why can't I abide in Christ every day, and every hour, and every moment? Why can't I have the light of my Father's love filling my heart all the day long? Tell me, servant of God, what can help me?"

I can tell you one thing that will help you. What helped Peter? "Peter went out and wept bitterly." It must come with us to a conviction of sin; it must come with us to a real downright earnest repentance, or we never can get into the better life. We must stop complaining and confessing, "Yes, my life is not what it should be, and I will try to do better." That won't help you. What will help you? This, that you go down in despair to lie at the feet of Jesus, and that you begin with a very real and bitter shame to make confession, "Lord Jesus, have compassion upon me! For these many years I have been a Christian, but there are so many sins from which I have not cleansed myself— temper, pride, jealousy, envy, sharp words, unkind judgments, unforgiving thoughts." One person must say, "There is a friend whom I never have forgiven for what he has said." Another must say, "There is an enemy whom I dislike; I cannot say that I can love him." Another must say, "There are things in my business that I would not like brought out into the light of man." Another must say, "I am led captive by the law of sin and death." Oh, Christians, come and make confession with shame and say, "I have been bought with the blood, I have been washed with the blood, but just think of what a life I have been living! I am ashamed of it." Bow before God and ask Him by the Holy Spirit to make you more deeply ashamed and to work in you that divine contrition. I pray you take the step at once. "Peter went out and wept bitterly," and that was his salvation; yes, that was the turning point of his life. And shall we not fall upon our faces before God, and make confession, and get down on our knees under the burden of the terrible load, and say, "I know I am a believer, but I am not living as I should to the glory of my God. I am under the power of the flesh and all the self-confidence, and self-will, and self-pleasing that marks my life."

Dear Christians, do you not long to be brought nigh unto God? Would you not give anything to walk in close fellowship with Jesus every day? Would you not count it a pearl of great price to have the light and love of God shining in you all the day? Oh, come and fall down and make confession of sin; and if you will do it, Jesus will come and meet you, and He will ask you, "Lovest thou Me?" And, if you say, "Yes, Lord," very quickly He will ask again, "Lovest thou Me?" And if you say, "Yes, Lord," again, He will ask a third time, "Lovest thou Me?" And your heart will be filled with an unutterable sadness, and your heart will get still more broken down and bruised by the question, and you will say, "Lord, I have not lived as I should, but still I love Thee and I give myself to Thee." O beloved, may God give us grace now, that, with Peter, we may go out and, if need be, weep bitterly. If we do not weep bitterly—we are not going to force tears—shall we not sigh very deeply, and bow very humbly, and cry very earnestly, "O God, reveal to me the carnal life in which I have been living: reveal to me what has been hindering me from having my life full of the Holy Ghost"? Shall we not cry, "Lord, break my heart into utter self-despair, and, oh, bring me in helplessness to wait for the divine power, for the power of the Holy Ghost, to take possession and to fill me with a new life given all to Jesus"?

OUT OF,
AND INTO

OUT OF,
AND INTO

And he brought us out from thence, that he might bring us in, to give us the land which he sware unto our fathers (Deut. 6:23).

 HAVE spoken of the crisis that comes in the life of the man who sees that his Christian experience is low and carnal and who desires to enter into the full life of God. Some Christians do not understand that there should be such a crisis. They think that they ought, from the day of their conversion, to continue to grow and progress. I have no objections to that, if they have grown as they ought. If their life has been so strong under the power of the Holy Ghost that they have grown as true believers should grow, I certainly have no objections to this. But I want to deal with those Christians whose life since conversion has been very much a failure and who feel it to be such because of their not being filled with the Spirit, as is their blessed privilege. I want to say, for their encouragement, that by taking one step, they can get out into the life of rest, and victory, and fellowship with God to which the promises of God invite them.

Look at the elder son in the parable (Luke 15). How long would it have taken him to get out of that state of blindness and bondage into the full condition of sonship? By believing in his father's love, he might have gotten out that very hour. If he had been powerfully convicted of his guilt in his unbelief and then had confessed like his prodigal brother, "I have sinned," he would have come that very moment into the favor of his loving father, and the enjoyment of the son's happiness in his father's home. He would not have been detained by having a great deal to learn and a great deal to do; in one moment his whole relation would have been changed.

Remember, too, what we saw in Peter's case. In one moment the look of Jesus broke him down, and there came to him the terribly bitter reflection of his sin, owing to his selfish, fleshly confidence, a contrition and reflection that laid the foundation for his new and better life with Jesus. God's Word brings out the idea of the Christian's entrance into the new and better life by the history of the people of Israel's entrance into the land of Canaan.

In our text we have these words: "[God] brought us out from thence [Egypt], that he might bring us in [into Canaan]." There are two steps: one was bringing them out, and the other was bringing them in. So in the life of the believer, there are ordinarily two steps quite separate from each other—the bringing him out of sin and the world and the bringing him into a state of complete rest afterward. It was the intention of God that Israel should enter the land of Canaan from Kadesh-Barnea immediately after He had made His covenant with them at Sinai. But they were not ready to enter at once, on account of their sin—unbelief and disobedience. They had to wander after that for forty years in the wilderness. Now, look how God led the people. In Egypt, there was a great crisis, where they had first to pass through the Red Sea, which is a figure of conversion; and when they went into Canaan, there was, as it were, a second conversion in passing through the Jordan. At our conversion, we get into liberty, out of the bondage of Egypt; but, when we fail to use our liberty through unbelief and disobedience, we wander in the wilderness for a longer or shorter period before we enter into Canaan—victory, rest, and abundance. Thus, God does for His Israel two things: He brings them out of Egypt, and He leads them into Canaan.

My message, then, is to ask this question of the believer: Since you know you are converted and God has brought you out of Egypt, have you yet come into the land of Canaan? If not, are you willing that He should bring you into the fuller liberty and rest provided for His people? He brought Israel out of Egypt by a mighty hand, and the same mighty hand brought us out of our land of bondage; with the same mighty hand, He brought his ancient people into rest, and by that hand, too, He can bring us into our true rest. The same God who pardoned and regenerated us—He who gives His love into our hearts—is waiting to perfect His love in us, if we but trust Him. Are there many hearts saying: "I believe that God brought me out of bondage twenty, or thirty, or forty years ago; but, alas, I cannot say that I have ever been brought into the happy land of rest and victory"?

How glorious was the rest of Canaan after all the wanderings in the wilderness! And so is it with the Christian who reaches the better promised Canaan of rest, when he comes to leave all his charge with the Lord Jesus—his responsibilities, anxieties, and worry—his only work being to hand the keeping of his soul into the hand of Jesus every day and hour. God can keep us and can give the victory over every enemy. Jesus has undertaken not only to cleanse our sin and bring us to heaven but also to keep us in our daily life.

I ask again, Are you hungering to get free from sin and its power? longing to get complete victory over temper, pride, and all evil inclinations? longing for the time when no clouds will come between you and your God? longing to walk in the full sunshine of God's loving favor? The very God who brought you from the Egypt of darkness is ready and able to bring you also into the Canaan of rest.

And now comes the question again: What is the way by which God will bring me to this rest? What is needed on my part if God is really to bring me into the happy land? I give the answer first of all by asking another question: Are you willing to forsake your wanderings in the wilderness? If you say, "We do not want to leave our wanderings, where we have had so many wonderful indications of God's presence with us, so many remarkable proofs of the divine care and goodness—like those of the ancient people of God, who had the pillar to guide them, the manna given them every day for forty years, Moses and Aaron to lead and advise them. The wilderness is to us, on account of these things, a kind of sacred place; and we are loth to leave it." If the children of Israel had said anything of this kind to Joshua, he would have said to them (and we all would have said): "Oh, you fools: It is the very God who gave you the pillar of cloud and the other blessings in the wilderness, who tells you now to come into the land flowing with milk and honey." And so I can speak to you in the same way; I bring you the message that He who has brought you thus far on your journey and given you such blessings thus far is the God who will bring you into the Canaan of complete victory and rest.

The first question, then, that I would ask you is,

ARE YOU READY TO LEAVE THE WILDERNESS?

You know the mark of Israel's life in the wilderness—the cause of all their troubles there—was unbelief. They did not believe that God could take them into the Promised Land. And then followed many sins and failures—lusting, idolatry, murmuring, etc. That has, perhaps, been your life, beloved; you do not believe that God will fulfill His Word. You do not believe in the possibility of unbroken fellowship and unlimited partnership with Him. On account of that, you became disobedient and did not live like a child doing God's will, because you did not believe that God could give you the victory over sin. Are you willing now to leave that wilderness life? Sometimes you are, perhaps, enjoying fellowship with God, and sometimes you are separated from Him; sometimes you have nearness to Him, at other times great distance from Him; sometimes you have a willingness to walk closely with Him, but sometimes there is even unwillingness. Are you now going to give up your whole life to Him? Are you going to approach Him and say, "My God, I do not want to do anything that will be displeasing to Thee; I want Thee to keep me from all worldliness, from all self-pleasing; I want Thee, O God, to help me to live like Peter after Pentecost, filled with the Holy Ghost, and not like carnal Peter"?

Beloved, are you willing to say this? Are you willing to give up your sins, to walk with God, continually to submit yourself wholly to the will of God, and have no will of your own apart from His will? Are you going to live a perfect life? I hope you are, for I believe in such a life, not perhaps in the sense in which you understand "perfection"—entire freedom from wrongdoing and all inclination to it—for while we live in the flesh the flesh will lust against the Spirit and the Spirit against the flesh, but the perfection spoken of in the Old Testament as practiced by some of God's saints, who are said to have "served the Lord with a perfect heart." What is this perfection? A state in which your hearts will be set on perfect integrity without any reserve and your will wholly subservient to God's will. Are you willing for such a perfection, with your whole heart turned away from the world and given to God alone? Are you going to say, "No, I do not expect that I will ever give up my self-will"? It is the devil tempting you to think it will be too hard for you.

Oh, I would plead with God's children just to look at the will of God, so full of blessing, of holiness, of love; will you not give up your guilty will for that blessed will of God? A man can do it in one moment when he comes to see that God can change his will for him. Then he may say farewell to his old will, as Peter did when he went out and wept bitterly and when the Holy Spirit filled his soul on the day of Pentecost. Joshua failed, indeed, before the enemy at Ai, because he trusted too much to human agency and not sufficiently to God; and he failed in the same manner when he made a covenant with the Gibeonites; but, still, his spirit and power differed very widely from that of the people whose unbelief drove them before their enemies and kept them in the wilderness. Let us be willing wholly to serve the Lord our God, and "make not provision for the flesh, to fulfill the lusts thereof." Let us believe in the love and power of God to keep us day by day, and let us "have no confidence in the flesh."

The second question is,

DO YOU BELIEVE THAT SUCH A LIFE IN THE LAND OF CANAAN IS POSSIBLE?

Many will say, "Ah! what would I give to get out of the wilderness life! But I cannot believe that it is possible to live in this constant communion with God. You don't know my difficulties, business cares, and perplexities; I have all sorts of people to associate with; have gone out in the morning braced up by communion with God in prayer, but the pressure of business before night has driven out of my heart all that warmth of love that I had, and the world has gotten in and made the heart as cold as before." But we must remember again what it was that kept Israel out of Canaan. When Caleb and Joshua said that Israel could overcome the enemy, the ten spies reported, "We be not able to go up against the people; for they are stronger than we." Take care, dear reader, that we do not repeat their sin, and provoke God as these unbelievers did. He says that it is possible to bring us into the land of rest and peace; and I believe it because He has said so and because He will do it if I trust Him. Your temper may be terrible; your pride may have bound you a hundred times; your temptations may "compass you about like bees," but there is victory for you if you will but trust the promises of God.

Look again at Peter. He had failed again and again and went from bad to worse, finally denying Christ

with oaths. But what a change came over him! Just
study the First Epistle of Peter, and you will see that the
very life of Christ had entered into him. He shows the
spirit of true humility, so different from his former self-
confidence, glorying in God's will instead of in his
own. He had made a full surrender to Christ and was
trusting entirely in Him. Come therefore today and say
to God, "Thou didst so change selfish, proud Peter,
and Thou canst change me likewise." Yes, God is able
to bring you into Canaan, the land of rest.

You know the first half of Romans 8. Notice the
expressions that are to be found there: "The law of the
Spirit of life in Christ Jesus hath made me free from the
law of sin and death," to walk after the Spirit, to be
after the Spirit, to be in the Spirit, to have the Spirit
dwelling in us, through the Spirit to mortify the deeds
of the body, to be led by the Spirit, to be spiritually
minded. These are all blessings that come when we
bind ourselves wholly to live in the Spirit. If we live
after the Spirit, we have the very nature of the Spirit in
us. If we live in the Spirit, we shall be led by Him every
day and every moment. What if you were to open your
heart today to be filled with the Holy Spirit? Would He
not be able to keep you every moment in the sweet rest
of God? and would not His mighty arm give you a
complete victory over sin and temptation of every kind
and make you able to live in perpetual fellowship with
the Father and with His Son, Jesus Christ? Most
certainly! This, then, is the second step; this is the
blessed life God has provided for us. First, God brought
us out of Egypt; secondly, He brings us into Canaan.

Then comes the third question,

HOW DOES GOD BRING US IN?

By leading us in a very definite act, viz., that of
committing ourselves wholly to Him—entrusting our-

selves to Him, that He may bring us into the land of rest and keep us in.

You remember that the Jordan at the time of harvest overflowed its banks. The hundreds of thousands of Israelites were on the east side of the river— outside of Canaan. They were told that tomorrow, God would do wonderful things for them. The trumpet would sound, and the priests would take up the ark— the symbol of God's presence—and pass over before the people. But there lay the swollen river still. If there were still unbelieving children among the people, they would say, "What fools, to attempt to cross now! This is not the time to attempt fording the river, for it is now twenty feet deep." But the believing people gathered together behind the priests with the ark. They obeyed the command of Joshua to advance; but they knew not what God was going to do. The priests walked right into the water, and the hearts of some began to tremble. They would perhaps ask, "Where is the rod of Moses?" But, as the priests walked straight on and stepped into the water, the waters rose up on the upper side in to a high wall and flowed away on the other side, and a clear passage was made for the whole camp. Now, it was God that did this for the people; and it was because Joshua and the people believed and obeyed God. The same God will do it today, if we believe and trust Him.

Perhaps I am addressing a soul who is saying, "I remember how God first brought me out of the land of bondage. I was in complete darkness of soul and was deeply troubled. I did not at first believe that God could take me out and that I could become a child of God. But, at last, God took me and brought me to trust in Jesus, and He led me out safely." Friend, you have the same God now who brought you out of bondage with a high hand and can lead you into the place of rest. Look to Him and say, "O God, make an end of my wilderness life—my sinful and unbelieving life—a life of grieving Thee. Oh, bring me today into the land of victory and rest and blessing!" Is this the prayer of your hearts, dear friends? Are you going to give up yourselves to Him to do this for you? Can you trust Him that He is able and willing to do it for you? He can take you through the swollen river this very moment, yes, *this very moment.*

And He can do more. After Israel had crossed the river, the Captain of the Lord's host had to come and encourage Joshua, promising to take charge of the army and remain with them. You need the power of God's Spirit to enable you to overcome sin and temptation. You need to live in His fellowship—in His unbroken fellowship, without which you cannot stand or conquer. If you are to venture today, say by faith, "My God, I know that Jesus Christ is willing to be the Captain of my salvation and to conquer every enemy for me. He will keep me by faith and by His Holy Spirit; and though it be dark to me, as if the waters would pass over my soul, and though my condition seem hopeless, I will walk forward, for God is going to bring me in today, and I am going to follow Him. My God, I follow Thee *now* into the promised land."

Perhaps some have already entered in, and the angels have seen them, while they have been reading these solemn words. Is there anyone still hesitating because the waters of Jordan look threatening and impassable?

Oh, come, beloved soul; come at once, and doubt not.

THE BLESSING
SECURED

THE BLESSING SECURED

Be filled with the Spirit (Eph. 5:18).

MAY have some air, a little air, in my lungs, but not enough to keep up a healthy, vigorous life. But everyone seeks to have his lungs well filled with air, and the benefit of it will be felt in his blood and through his whole being. And just so the Word of God comes to us and says, "Christians, do not be content with thinking you *have* the Spirit or with having a *little* of the Spirit; but, if you want to have a healthy life, be '*filled* with the Spirit.'" Is that your life? Or are you ready to cry out, "Alas, I do not know what it is to be filled with the Spirit, but it is what I long for"? I want to point out to such the path to this great, precious blessing that is meant for every one of us.

Before I speak further of it, let me just note one misunderstanding that prevails. People often look upon being "filled with the Spirit" as something that comes with a mighty stirring of the emotions, a sort of heavenly glory that comes over them, something that they can feel strongly and mightily; but that is not always the case. I was recently at Niagara Falls. I noticed, and I was told, that the water was unusually low. Suppose the river were doubly full, how would you see that fulness in the Falls? In the increased volume of water pouring over the cataract and in its tremendous noise. But go to another part of the river, or to the lake, where the very same fulness is found, and there is perfect quiet and placidity, the rise of the water is gentle and gradual, and you can hardly notice that there is any disturbance as the lake gets full. And just so it may be with a child of God. To one it comes with mighty emotion and with a blessed consciousness, "God has touched me!" To others it comes in a gentle filling of the whole being with the presence and the power of God by His Spirit. I do not want to lay down the way in which it is to come to you, but I want you simply to take your place before God, and say, "My Father, whatever it may mean, that is what I want." If you come and give yourself up as an empty vessel and trust God to fill you, God will do His own work.

And now, the simple question as to the steps by which we can come to be "filled with the Spirit." I shall note four steps in the way by which a man can attain this wonderful blessing. He must say, (1) "I *must* have it," then, (2) "I *may* have it," then, (3) "I *will* have it," and then, (4) "Thank God, I *shall* have it."

The first word a man must begin to say is, "I *must* have it." He must feel "It is a command of God, and I cannot live unfilled with the Spirit without disobeying God." It is a command here in this text, "Be not drunk with wine, but be *filled with the Spirit*." Just as much as a man dare not get drunk, if he is a Christian, just as much must a man be filled with the Spirit. God wants it, and oh, that every one might be brought to say, "I must, if I am to please God, I must be filled with the Spirit!"

I fear there is a terrible, terrible self-satisfaction among many Christians; they are content with their low level of life. They think they have the Spirit because they are converted, but they know very little of the joy of the Holy Ghost and of His sanctifying power. They know very little of the fellowship of the Spirit linking them to God and to Jesus. They know very little of the power of the Spirit to testify for God, and yet they are content; and one says, "Oh, it is only for eminent Christians." A very dear young friend once said to me as I was talking to her (it was a niece of my own), "Oh, Uncle Andrew, I cannot try to make myself better than the Christians around me. Wouldn't that be presumptuous?" And I said, "My child, you must not ask what the Christians around you are, but you must be guided by what God says." She has since confessed to me how bitterly ashamed she has become of that expression and how she went to God to seek His blessing. Oh, friends, do not be content with that half-Christian life that many of you are living, but say, "God wants it, God commands it; I *must* be filled with the Spirit."

And look not only at God's command, but look at the need of your own soul. You are a parent, and you want your children blessed and converted, and you complain that you haven't power to bless them. You say, "My home must be filled with God's Spirit." You complain of your own soul, of times of darkness and of leanness; you complain of watchlessness and wandering. A young minister once said to me, "Oh, why is it I have such a delight in study and so little delight in prayer?" My answer was, "My brother, your heart must get filled with a love for God and Jesus, and then you will delight in prayer." You complain sometimes that you cannot pray. You pray so short, you do not know what to pray, something drags you back from the closet. It is because you are living a life, trying to live a life, without being *filled* with the Spirit. Oh, think of the needs of the church around you. You are a Sunday school teacher; you are trying to teach a class of ten or twelve children, not one of them, perhaps, converted, and they go out from under you unconverted; you are trying to do a heavenly work in the power of the flesh and earth. Sunday school teachers, do begin to say, "I *must* be filled with the Spirit of God, or I must give up the charge of those young souls; I cannot teach them."

Or, think of the need of the world. If you were to send out missionaries full of the Holy Ghost, what a blessing that would be! Why is it that many a missionary complains in the foreign field, "There I learned how weak and how unfit I am"? It is because the churches from which they go are not filled with the Holy Ghost. Someone said to me in England a few weeks ago, "They talk so much about the volunteer movement and more missionaries, but we want something else; we want missionaries filled with the Holy Ghost." If the church is to come right, and the mission field is to come right, we must each begin with himself. It must begin with *you*. Begin with yourself and say, "O God, for Thy sake; O God, for Thy church's sake; O God, for the sake of the world, help me! I *must* be filled with the Holy Ghost."

What folly it would be for a man who had lost a

lung and a half, and had hardly a half of a lung to do the work of two, to expect to be a strong man and to do hard work and to live in any climate! And what folly for a man to expect to live—God has told him he cannot live—a full Christian life, unless he is full of the Holy Ghost! And what folly for a man who has only got a little drop of the river of the water of life to expect to live and to have power with God and man! Jesus wants us to come and to receive the fulfilment of the promise, "He that believeth in Me, streams of water shall flow out from him." Oh, begin to say, "If I am to live a right life, if I am in every part of my daily life and conduct to glorify my God, I must have the Holy Spirit—I must be filled with the Spirit." Are you going to say that? Talking for months and months won't help. Do submit to God, and as an act of submission say, "Lord, I confess it, I ought to be filled, I *must* be filled; help me!" And God will help you.

And, then comes the second step, I *may* be filled. The first had reference to duty; the second has reference to privilege—I *may* be filled. Alas! So many have got accustomed to their low state that they do not believe that they may, they can, actually be filled. And what right have I to say that you ought to take these words to your lips? My right is this: God wants healthy children. I saw today a child of six months old, as beautiful and chubby as you could wish a child to be, and with what delight the eyes of the father and the mother looked upon him; and how glad I was to see a healthy child. And, oh, do you think that God in heaven does not care for His children, that God wants some of His children to live a sickly life? I tell you, it is a lie! God wants every child of His to be a healthy Christian; but you cannot be a healthy Christian unless you are filled with God's Spirit. Beloved, we have got accustomed to a style of life, and we see good Christians—as we call them—earnest men and women, full of failings; and we think, "Well, that is human; that man loses his temper, and that man is not as kind as he should be, and that man's word cannot be trusted always as ought to be the case; but . . . ." And in daily life we look upon Christians and think, "All is well, if they are very faithful in going to church, and in giving to God's cause, and in attending the prayer meeting, and in having family prayers, and in their profession." Of course, we thank God for them and say, "We wish there were more such," but we forget to ask, "What does God want?" Oh, that we might see that it is meant for me and for everyone else. My brother, my sister, there is a God in heaven who has been longing for these past years, while you never thought about it, to fill you with the Holy Ghost. God longs to give the fulness of the Spirit to every child of His.

They were poor heathen Ephesians, only lately brought out from heathendom, to whom Paul wrote this letter—people among whom there still was stealing and lying, for they had only just come out from heathendom; but Paul said to every one of these, "Be filled with the Spirit." God is ready to do it; God wants to do it. Oh, do not listen to the temptation of the devil, "This is only meant for some eminent people— Christians who have a great deal of free time to devote to prayer and to seeking after it, those with a receptive temperament—they are the ones to be filled with the Spirit." Who is there that dare say, "I cannot be filled with the Spirit"? Who will dare to say that? If any of you speak thus, it is because you are unwilling to give up sin. Do not think that you cannot be filled with the

Spirit because God is not willing to give it to you. Did not the Lord Jesus promise the Spirit? Is not the Holy Spirit the best part of His salvation? Do you think He gives half a salvation to any of His redeemed ones? Is not His promise for all, "He that believeth in Me, rivers of water shall flow out of him"? This is more than fulness—this is overflow; and this Jesus has promised to everyone who believes in Him. Oh, cast aside your fears, and your doubts, and your hesitation, and say at once, "I *can* be filled with the Spirit, I *may* be filled with the Spirit. There is nothing in heaven, or earth, or hell, that can prevent it, because God has promised and God is waiting to do it for me." Are you ready to say, "I *may*, I *can* be filled with the Spirit, for God has promised it, and God will give it"?

And then we get to the third step, when a man says, "I *will* have it; I *must* have it; I *may* have it." You know what "I *will* have it" means in ordinary things; he goes and does everything that is to be done to get possession. Very often a man comes and wants to buy something, and he wishes for it; but *wishing* is not *willing*. I want to buy that horse, and a man asks of me $200 for it, but I don't want to give more than $180. I wish for it, I wish it very much, and I can go and say, "Do give it me for the $180." And he says, "No, $200." I love the horse, it is just what I want, but I am not willing to give the $200; and at last he says, "Well, you must give me an answer; I can get another purchaser." And at last I say, "No, I won't have it; I want it very much, I long for it, but I won't give the price."

Dear friends, are you going to say, "I *will* have this blessing"? What does that mean? It means, first of all, of course, that you are going to give up every sin, you are going to look around into your life; and if you see anything wrong there, it means that you are going to confess it to Jesus and say, "Lord, I cast it at Thy feet; it may be rooted in my heart, but I will give it up to Thee. I cannot take it out, but Jesus, Thou cleanser of sin, I give it to Thee." Let it be temper, or pride; let it be money, or lust, or pleasure; let it be the fear of man; let it be anything. But, oh, say to Christ at once, "I will have this blessing at any cost." Oh, give up every sin to Jesus.

And it means not only giving up every sin, but—what is deeper than sin, and more difficult to get at—it means giving up yourself—self, with your will, and your pleasure, and your honor, and all you have, and saying, "Jesus, I am from this moment going to give myself up, that by Thy Holy Spirit Thou mayest take possession of me, and that Thou mayest by Thy Spirit turn out whatever is sinful and take entire command of me." This looks difficult so long as Satan blinds and makes us think it would be a hard thing to give up all that; but if God opens our eyes for one minute to see what a heavenly blessedness and what heavenly riches and heavenly glory it is to be filled with the Spirit out of the heart of Jesus, then we will say, "I will give anything, *anything*, ANYTHING, but I *will* have the blessing."

And then, it means that you are just to cast yourself at His feet and to say, "Lord, I *will* have the blessing."

Ah, Satan often tempts us, and says, "Suppose God were to ask that of you, would you be willing to give it?" And he makes us afraid. But how many have found, and have been able to tell about it, that when once they have said, "Lord, anything and everything!" the light and the joy of heaven filled their hearts.

Last year at Johannesburg, the gold fields of South Africa, we had one day a time for testimony at an afternoon meeting. A woman rose up and told us how her pastor two months before had held a consecration service in a tent; he had spoken strongly about consecration and had said, "Now, if God were to send your husband away to China, or if God were to ask you to go away to America, would you be willing for it? You must give yourself up entirely." And the woman said— and her face beamed with brightness when she spoke— when, at the close of the meeting, he asked those to rise who were willing to give up all to be filled with the Spirit, she had thought, "The struggle is terrible; God may take away my husband or my children from me, and am I ready for it? Oh, Jesus is very precious, but I cannot say I will give up all. But I will tell Him I do want to do it." At last she had stood up. She said she went home that night in a terrible struggle, and she could not sleep, for the thought was, "I said to Jesus *everything*, and could I give up husband or child?" The struggle continued till midnight, "but," she said, "I would not let go; I said to Jesus, 'everything, but fill me with Thyself.'" And the joy of the Holy Spirit came down upon her, and her minister who sat there told me afterwards that the testimony was a true one and that for the two months her life had been one of exceeding brightness and of heavenly joy.

Oh, is any reader tempted to say, "I cannot give up all"? I take you by the hand, my brother, my sister, and I bring you to the crucified Jesus, and I say, "Just look at Him, how He loved you on Calvary; just look at Him." Just look at Jesus! He offers actually to fill your heart with His Holy Spirit, with the Spirit of His love and of His fulness, and of His power, actually to make your heart full of the Holy Spirit; and do you dare to say, "I am afraid"? Do you dare to say, "I cannot do that for Jesus"? Or will your heart not, at His feet, cry out, "Lord Jesus, anything, but I *must* be filled with Thy Spirit!" Haven't you often prayed for the presence and the abiding nearness and the love of Jesus to fill you? But that cannot be until you are filled with the Holy Spirit. Oh, come and say, in view of any sacrifice, "I *will* have it, by God's help! Not in *my* strength, but by the help of God, I will have it!"

And then comes my last point. Say, "I *shall* have it." Praise God that a man dare say, "I shall have it." Yes, when a man has made up his mind—when a man has been brought to a conviction and a sorrow for his sinful life—when a man, like Peter, has wept bitterly or has sighed deeply before God, "O my Lord, what a life I have been living!"—when a man has felt wretched in the thought, "I am not living the better life, the Jesus life, the Spirit life"—when a man begins to feel that, and when he comes and makes surrender, and casts himself upon God and claims the promise, "Lord, I may have it; it is for me"—what think you? Hasn't he a right to say, "I *shall* have it"? Yes, beloved, and I give to every one of you that message from God, that if you are willing, and if you are ready, God is willing and ready to close the bargain at once. Yes, you can have it now, *now*, NOW! Without any outburst of feeling, without any flooding of the heart with light, you may have it. To some it comes in that way, to some not. As a quiet transaction of the surrendered will, you can lift up your heart in faith and say, "O God, here I do give myself as an empty vessel to be filled with the Holy Ghost. I give myself up once for all and forever. 'Tis done, the great transaction's done.'" You can say it now if you will take your place before God.

Oh, ministers of the gospel, have you never felt the need of being filled with the Holy Ghost? Your heart perhaps tells you that you know nothing of that blessing. Oh, workers for Christ, have you never felt a need, "I must be filled with the Holy Ghost"? Oh, children of God, have you never felt a hope rise within you, "I may have this blessing I hear of from others"? Will you not take the step and say, "I will have it"? Say it, not in your own strength, but in self-despair. Never mind though it appears as if the heart is all cold and closed up, never mind; but as an act of obedience and of surrender, as an act of the will, cast yourself before Jesus and trust Him. "I *shall* have it, for I now give up myself into the arms of my Lord Jesus; I *shall* have it, for it is the delight of Jesus to give the Holy Spirit from the Father into the heart of everyone. I *shall* have it, for I do believe in Jesus, and He promised me that out of him that believeth shall flow rivers of living water. I *shall* have it! I SHALL have it! I will cling to the feet of Jesus, I will stay at the throne of God; I *shall* have it, for God is faithful, and God has promised."

THE PRESENCE
OF CHRIST

THE PRESENCE
OF CHRIST

But straightway Jesus spake unto them saying, Be of good cheer; it is I; be not afraid (Matt. 14:27).

LL we have had about the work of the blessed Spirit is dependent upon what we think of Jesus, for it is *from* Christ Jesus that the Spirit comes to us; it is *to* Christ Jesus that the Spirit ever brings us; and the one need of the Christian life day by day and hour by hour is this: the presence of the Son of God. God is our salvation. If I have Christ with me and Christ in me, I have full salvation. We have spoken about the life of failure and of the flesh, about the life of unbelief and disobedience, about the life of ups and downs, the wilderness life of sadness and of sorrow; but we have heard, and we have believed, there is deliverance. Bless God, He brought us out of Egypt, that He might bring us into Canaan, into the very rest of God and Jesus Christ. He is our peace, He is our rest. Oh, if I may only have the presence of Jesus as the victory over every sin—the presence of Jesus as the strength for every duty—then my life shall be in the full sunshine of God's unbroken fellowship, and the word will be fulfilled to me in most blessed experience, "Son, thou art ever with me, and all I have is thine," and my heart shall answer, "Father, I never knew it, but it is true—I am ever with Thee, and all Thou hast is mine." God has given all He has to Christ, and God longs that Christ should have you and me entirely. I come to every hungry heart and say, "If you want to live to the glory of God, seek one thing: to claim, to believe, that the presence of Jesus can be with you every moment of your life."

I want to speak about the presence of Jesus as it is set before us in that blessed account of Christ's walking on the sea. Come and look with me at some points that are suggested to us.

Think, first, of the presence of Christ *lost*. You know the disciples loved Christ, clung to Him, and with all their failings delighted in Him. But what happened? The Master went up into the mountain to pray, and sent them across the sea all alone without Him; there came a storm, and they toiled, rowed, and labored, but the wind was against them. They made no progress, they were in danger of perishing, and how their hearts said, "Oh, if the Master only were here!" But His presence was gone. They missed Him. Once before, they had been in a storm, and Christ had said, "Peace, be still," and all was well; but here they are in darkness, danger, and terrible trouble, and no Christ to help them. Ah, isn't that the life of many a believer at times? I get into darkness, I have committed sin, the cloud is on me, I miss the face of Jesus; and for days and days I work, worry, and labor; but it is all in vain, for I miss the presence of Christ. Oh, beloved, let us write that down: the presence of Jesus lost is the cause of all our wretchedness and failure.

Look at the second step—the presence of Jesus *dreaded*. They were longing for the presence of Christ, and Christ came after midnight. He came walking on the water amid the waves, but they didn't recognize Him, and they cried out for fear, "It is a spirit!" Their beloved Lord was coming nigh, and they knew Him not. They dreaded His approach. And, ah, how often have I seen a believer dreading the approach of Christ— crying out for Him, longing for Him, and yet dreading His coming. And why? Because Christ came in a fashion that they expected not.

Perhaps some have been saying, "Alas, alas! I fear I never can have the abiding presence of Christ." You have heard what we have said about a life in the Spirit; you have heard what we have said about abiding ever in the presence of God and in His fellowship, and you have been afraid of it, afraid of it, and have said, "It is too high and too difficult." You have dreaded the very teaching that was going to help you. Jesus came to you in the teaching, and you didn't recognize His love.

Or, perhaps, He came in a way that you dreaded His presence. Perhaps God has been speaking to you about some sin. There is that sin of temper, or that sin of unlovingness, or that sin of unforgivingness, or that sin of worldliness, compromise, and fellowship with the world, that love of man and man's honor, that fear of man and man's opinion, or that pride and self-confidence. God has been speaking to you about it, and yet you have been frightened. That was Jesus wanting to draw you nigh, but you were afraid. You don't see how you can give up all that, you are not ready to say,

"At any sacrifice I am going to have that taken out of me, and I *will* give it up," and while God was coming nigh to bless you, you were afraid of Him.

Oh, believers, at other times Christ has come to you with affliction, and perhaps you have said, "If I want to be entirely holy, I know I shall have to be afflicted, and I am afraid of affliction," and you have dreaded the thought, "Christ may come to me in affliction." The presence of Christ dreaded! Oh, beloved, I want to tell you it is all misconception. The disciples had no reason to dread that "spirit" coming there, for it was Christ Himself; and, when God's Word comes close to you and touches your heart, remember that is Christ out of whose mouth goes the two-edged sword. It is Christ in His love, coming to cut away the sin so that He may fill your heart with the blessing of God's love. Beware of dreading the presence of Christ.

Then comes the third thought—the presence of Christ *revealed*. Bless God! When Christ heard how they cried, He spoke the words of the text, "Be of good cheer; it is I; be not afraid." Ah, what gladness those words brought to those hearts! There is Jesus, that dark object, that dreaded form. It is our blessed Lord Himself. And, dear friends, the Master's object, whether it be by affliction or otherwise, is to prepare us for receiving the presence of Christ, and through it all Jesus speaks, "It is I; be not afraid." The presence of Christ revealed! I want to tell you that the Son of God, O believer, is longing to reveal Himself to you. Listen! *Listen*! LISTEN! Is there any longing heart? Jesus says, "Be of good cheer; it is I; be not afraid."

O beloved, God has given us Christ. And does God want me to have Christ every moment? Without doubt. God wants the presence of Christ to be the joy of every hour of my life; and if there is one thing sure, Christ can reveal Himself to me every moment. Are you willing to come and claim this privilege? He can reveal Himself. I cannot reveal Him to you; you cannot grasp Him; but He can shine into your heart. How can I see the sunlight tomorrow morning, if I am spared? The sunlight will reveal itself. How can I know Christ? Christ can reveal Himself. And, ere I go further, I pray you to set your heart upon this and to offer the humble prayer, "Lord, now reveal Thyself to me, so that I may never lose the sight of Thee. Give me to understand that through the thick darkness Thou comest to make Thyself known." Let not one heart doubt, however dark it may be—at midnight, whatever midnight there be in the soul, at midnight, in the dark—Christ can reveal Himself. Ah, thank God, often after a life of ten and twenty years of dawn, after a life of ten and twenty years of struggling, now in the light, now in the dark, there comes a time when Jesus is willing just to give Himself to us, nevermore to part. God grant us that presence of Jesus!

And now comes the fourth thought. The presence of Jesus *lost* was the first; the presence of Jesus *dreaded* was the second; the presence of Jesus *revealed* was the third; and now the presence of Jesus *desired* is the fourth. What happened? Peter heard the Lord, and he was content. He was in the boat, and yonder was Jesus, some thirty, forty, fifty yards distant, and He made as though He would have passed them. In a preceding chapter I spoke about Peter, showing what terrible failure and carnality there was in him; but, bless the Lord, Peter's heart was right with Christ, and he wanted to claim His presence, and he said, "Lord, if it be Thou, bid me come upon the water to Thee." Yes, Peter could not rest; he wanted to be as near to Christ as possible. He saw Christ walking on the water; he remembered Christ had said, "Follow Me," remembered how Christ, with the miraculous draught of fishes, had proved that He was Master of the sea and of the waters, and remembered how Christ had stilled the storm; and, without argument or reflection, all at once he said, "There is my Lord manifesting Himself in a new way; there is my Lord exercising a new and supernatural power, and I can go to my Lord; He is able to make me walk where He walks." He wanted to walk like Christ; he wanted to walk near Christ. He didn't say, "Lord, let me walk around the sea here," but he said, "Lord, let me come to Thee."

Friends, would you not like to have the presence of Christ in this way? Not that Christ should come down. That is what many Christians want; they want to continue in their sinful walk, they want to continue in their worldly walk, they want to continue in their old life, and they want Christ to come down to them with His comfort, His presence, and His love; but that cannot be. If I am to have the presence of Christ, I must walk as He walked. His walk was a supernatural one. He walked in the love and in the power of God.

Most people walk according to the circumstances in which they are, and most people say, "I am depending upon circumstances for my religion." A hundred times over you hear people say, "My circumstances prevent my enjoying unbroken fellowship with Jesus." What were the circumstances that were around about Christ? The wind and the waves; and Christ walked triumphant over circumstances. Peter said, "Like my Lord I can triumph over all circumstances:

anything around me is nothing, if I have Jesus." He longed for the presence of Christ. Would God that, as we look at the life of Christ upon earth, as we look how Christ walked and conquered the waves, every one of us could say, "I want to walk like Jesus." If that is your heart's desire, you can expect the presence of Jesus; but as long as you want to walk on a lower level than Christ, as long as you want to have a little of the world and a little of self-will, do not expect to have the presence of Christ. Near Christ and like Christ—the two things go together. Have you taken that in? Peter wanted to walk like Christ that he might get near Christ; and it is this I want to offer every one of you. I want to say to the weakest believer, "With God's presence you can have the presence and fellowship of Christ all the day long, your whole life through." I want to bring you that promise, but I must give God's condition—walk like Christ, and you shall always abide near Christ. The presence of Christ invites you to come and have unbroken fellowship with Him.

Then comes the next thought. We have just had the presence of Christ desired; and my next thought is, the presence of Christ *trusted*. The Lord Jesus said, "Come," and what did Peter do? He stepped out of the boat. How did he dare to do it against all the laws of nature? How did he dare to do it? He sought Christ, he heard Christ's voice, he trusted Christ's presence and power, and with faith in Christ he said, "I can walk on the water," and he stepped out of the boat. Here is the turning point; here is the crisis. Peter saw Christ in the manifestation of a supernatural power, and Peter believed that supernatural power could work in him and he could live a supernatural life. He believed this applied to walking on the sea; and herein lies the whole secret of the life of faith. Christ had supernatural power—the power of heaven, the power of holiness, the power of fellowship with God—and Christ can give me grace to live as He lived. If I will but, like Peter, look at Christ and say to Christ, "Lord, speak the word, and I will come," and if I will listen to Christ saying, "Come," I, too, shall have power to walk upon the waves.

Have you ever seen a more beautiful and more instructive symbol of the Christian life? I once preached on it many years ago, and the thought that filled my heart then was this: the Christian life compared to Peter walking on the waves—nothing so difficult and impossible without Christ, nothing so blessed and safe with Christ. That is the Christian life—impossible without Christ's nearness, most safe and blessed, however difficult, if I only have the presence of Christ.

Believers, we have tried in these pages to call you to a better life, to a spiritual life, to a holy life, to a life in the Spirit, to a life in the fellowship with God. There is only one thing that can enable you to live it: you must have the Lord Jesus hold your hand every minute of the day. "But can that be?" you ask. Yes, it can. "I have so much to think of. Sometimes for four or five hours of the day I have to go into the very thick of business and have some ten men standing around me, each claiming my attention. How can I—how can I always—have the presence of Jesus?" Beloved, because Jesus is your God and loves you wonderfully, and is able to make His presence more clear to you than that of ten men who are standing around you. You must take time to enter into your covenant every morning with Him. If you will pray in the morning, "My Lord Jesus, nothing can satisfy me but Thine abiding presence," He will give it to you; He will surely give it to you. Oh, Peter trusted the presence of Christ, and he said, "If Christ calls me, I can walk on the waves to Him." Shall we trust the presence of Christ? To walk through all the circumstances and temptations of life is exactly like walking on the water—you have no solid ground under your feet, you do not know how strong the temptations of Satan may come. But do believe God wants you to walk in a supernatural life above human power; God wants you to live a life in Christ Jesus. Are you wanting to live that life? Come then, and say, "Jesus, I have heard Thy promise that Thy presence will go with me. Thou hast said, 'My presence shall go with thee,' and, Lord, I claim it; I trust Thee."

Now, the sixth step in this wonderful history—the presence of Christ *forgotten*. Peter got out of the boat and began to walk toward the Lord Jesus with his eye fixed upon Him. The presence of Christ was trusted by him, and he walked boldly over the waves; but all at once he took his eye off Jesus, and he began at once to sink; and there was Peter, his walk of faith at an end, all drenched and drowning and crying, "Lord, help me!" There are some of you saying in your hearts, I know, "Ah, that's what will come of your higher-life Christians." There are people who say, "You never can live that life; do not talk of it; you must always be failing." Peter always failed before Pentecost. It was because the Holy Spirit had not yet come; and therefore his experience goes to teach us, that while Peter was still in the life of the flesh he must fail somehow or other. But, thank God, there was One to lift him out of the failure; and our last point will be to prove that out of that failure he came into closer union with—and deeper dependence upon—Jesus than ever before. But listen, first, while I speak to you about this failure.

Someone may say, "I have been trying to say, 'Lord, I will live it.' But, tell me, suppose failure comes, what then?" Learn from Peter what you ought to do. What did Peter do? The very opposite of what most do. What did he do when he began to sink? That very moment, without one word of self-reproach or self-condemnation, he cried, "Lord, help me!" I wish I could teach every Christian that. I remember the time in my spiritual life when that became clear to me; for up to that time, when I failed, my only thought was to reproach and condemn myself, and I thought that would do me good. I found it didn't do me good; and I learn from Peter that my work is, the very moment I fail, to say, "Jesus, Master, help me!" and the very moment I say that, Jesus does help me. Remember, failure is not an impossibility. I can conceive that more than one Christian has said, "Lord, I claim the fulness of the Holy Ghost. I want to live every hour of every day filled with the Holy Spirit." And I can conceive that an honest soul said that with a trembling faith and yet may have fallen; I want to say to that soul, Don't be discouraged. If failure comes, at once, without any waiting, appeal to Jesus. He is always ready to hear, and the very moment you find there is the temper, the hasty word, or some other wrong, at once the living Jesus is near, so gracious and so mighty. Appeal to Him, and there will be help at once. If you will learn to do this, Jesus will lift you up and lead you on to a walk where His strength shall secure you from failure.

And then comes my last thought. The presence of Jesus was forgotten while Peter looked at the waves; but now, lastly, we have the presence of Jesus *restored*. Yes, Jesus stretched out His hand to save him. Possibly—for Peter was a very proud, self-confident man—

possibly he had to sink there to teach him that his faith could not save him; only the power of Christ could. God wants us to learn the lesson that when we fall, then we can cry to Jesus, and at once He reaches out His hand. Remember, Peter walked back to the boat without sinking again. Why? Because Christ was very near him. Remember, it is quite possible, if you use your failure rightly, to be far nearer Christ after it than before. Use it rightly, I say. That is, come and acknowledge, "In me there is nothing, but I am going to trust my Lord unboundedly." Let every failure teach you to cling afresh to Christ, and He will prove Himself a mighty and a loving Helper. The presence of Jesus restored! Yes, Christ took him by the hand and helped him, and I don't know whether they walked hand in hand those forty or fifty yards back to the boat or whether Christ allowed Peter to walk beside Him; but this I know, they were very near each other, and it was the nearness to his Lord that strengthened him.

Remember what has taken place since that happened with Peter. The cross has been erected, the blood has been shed, the grave has been opened, the resurrection has been accomplished, heaven has been opened, and the Spirit of the exalted Christ has come down. Do believe that it is possible for the presence of Jesus to be with us every day and all the way. Your God has given you Christ, and He wants to give you Christ into your heart in such a way that His presence shall be with you every moment of your life.

Who is willing to lift up his eyes and his heart and to exclaim, "I want to live according to God's standard?" Who is willing? Who is willing to cast himself into the arms of Jesus and to live a life of faith— victorious over the winds and the waves, over the circumstances and difficulties? Who is willing to say this, "Lord, bid me come to Thee upon the water"? Are you willing? Listen! Jesus says, "Come." Will you step out at this moment? Yonder is the boat, the old life that Peter had been leading; he had been familiar with the sea from his boyhood, and that boat was a very sacred place; Christ had sat beside him there; Christ had preached from that boat; from that boat of Peter's, Christ had given the wonderful draught of fishes; it was a very sacred boat; but Peter left it to come to a place more sacred still—walking with Jesus on the water, a new and a divine experience. Your Christian life may be a very sacred thing; you may say, "Christ saved me by His blood and has given me many an experience of grace; God has proved His grace in my heart. But," you confess, "I haven't got the real life of abiding fellowship; the winds and the waves often terrify me, and I sink."

Oh, come out of the boat of past experiences at once; come out of the boat of external circumstances; come out of the boat, and step out on the word of Christ, and believe, "With Jesus I can walk upon the water." When Peter was in the boat, what had he between him and the bottom of the sea? A couple of planks. But when he stepped out upon the water, what had he between him and the sea? Not a plank, but the word of the almighty Jesus. Will you come, and without any experience, will you rest upon the word of Jesus, "Lo, I am with you alway"? Will you rest upon His word, "Be of good cheer; fear not; it is I"? Every moment Jesus lives in heaven; every moment by His Spirit Jesus whispers that word; and every moment He lives to make it true. Accept it now, accept it now! My Lord Jesus is equal to every emergency. My Lord Jesus can meet the wants of every soul. My whole heart says, "He *can*, He *can* do it; He *will*, He *will* do it!" Oh come, believers, and let us claim—most deliberately, most quietly, most restfully—let us claim, claim it, *claim it*, CLAIM IT.

A WORD
TO WORKERS

A WORD
TO WORKERS

OME time ago I read this statement in an old author: "The first duty of every clergyman is to humbly ask God that all that he wants done in his hearers may be first fully and truly done in himself." These words have stuck with me ever since. What a solemn application this is to the subject that occupied our attention in previous chapters—the living and working under the fulness of the Holy Spirit! And yet, if we understand our calling aright, every one of us will have to admit that that is the one thing on which everything depends.

What profit is it to tell men that they may be filled with the Spirit of God, if, when they ask us, "Has God done it for you?" we have to answer, "No, He has not done it"? What profit is it for me to tell men that Jesus Christ can dwell within us every moment and keep us from sin and actual transgression, and that the abiding presence of God can be our portion all the day, if I personally wait not upon God first to do it truly and fully day by day?

Look at the Lord Jesus Christ; it was of the Christ Himself, when He had received the Holy Ghost from heaven, that John the Baptist said that He would baptize with the Holy Ghost. I can only communicate to others what God has imparted to me. If my life as a minister be a life in which the flesh still greatly prevails, if my life be a life in which I grieve the Spirit of God, I cannot expect but that my people will receive through me a very mingled kind of life. But if the life of God dwell in me, and I am filled with His power, then I can hope that the life that goes out from me may be infused into my hearers too.

We have referred to the need of every believer being filled with the Spirit; and what is there of deeper interest to us now, or that can better occupy our attention, than prayerfully to consider how we can bring our congregations to believe that this is possible and how we can lead on every believer to seek it for himself, to expect it, and to accept of it, so as to live it out? But, brethren, the message must come from us as a witness of our personal experience, by the grace of God.

The same writer to whom I alluded says elsewhere: "The first business of a clergyman, when he sees men awakened and brought to Christ, is to lead them on to know the Holy Spirit." How true! Do not we find this throughout the Word of God? John the Baptist preached Christ as the "Lamb of God, which taketh away the sin of the world." We read in Matthew that he also said that Christ would baptize with the Holy Ghost and with fire. In the Gospel of John, we read that the Baptist was told that upon whom he would see the Spirit descending and abiding, He it was who would baptize with the Spirit. Thus, John the Baptist led the

people on from Christ to the expectation of the Holy
Ghost for themselves. And what did Jesus do? For three
years, He was with His disciples, teaching and instruct-
ing them; but when He was about to go away, in His
farewell discourse on the last night, what was His great
promise to the disciples? "I will pray the Father, and he
shall give you another Comforter, . . . even the Spirit
of truth." He had previously promised to those who
believed on Him, that "rivers of living water" should
flow from them, which the Evangelist explains as
meaning the Holy Ghost: "Thus spake He of the
Spirit." But this promise was to be fulfilled only after
Christ "was glorified." Christ points to the Holy Spirit
as the one fruit of His being glorified. The glorified
Christ leads to the Holy Ghost. So in the farewell
discourse, Christ leads the disciples to expect the Spirit
as the Father's great blessing. Then again, when Christ
came and stood at the footstool of His heavenly throne,
on the Mount of Olives, ready to ascend, what were
His words? "Ye shall receive power, after that the Holy
Ghost is come upon you; and ye shall be witnesses unto
Me." Christ's constant work was to teach His disciples
to expect the Holy Spirit.

Look through the Book of Acts, and you see the
same thing. Peter on the day of Pentecost preached that
Christ was exalted and had received of the Father the
promise of the Holy Ghost; and so he told the people:
"Repent, and be baptized every one of you in the name
of Jesus Christ for the remission of sins, and ye shall
receive the gift of the Holy Ghost." So, anyone who
believes in the risen, ascended, and glorified Jesus will
receive the Holy Ghost.

Look further. After Philip had preached the gospel
in Samaria, men and women had been converted and

there was great joy in the city. The Holy Spirit had been working, but something was still wanting; Peter and John came down from Jerusalem, prayed for the converted ones, and laid their hands upon them, "and they received the Holy Ghost." Then they had the conscious possession and enjoyment of the Spirit; but till that came they were incomplete. Paul was converted by the mighty power of Jesus, who appeared to him on the way to Damascus; and yet he had to go to Ananias to be filled with the Holy Ghost.

Then again, we read that when Peter went to preach to Cornelius, as he preached Christ, "the Holy Ghost fell on all them which heard the word." Peter took this as the sign that these Gentiles were one with the Jews in the favor of God, having the same baptism.

And so we might go through many of the Epistles, where we find the same truth taught. Look at that wonderful Epistle to the Romans. The doctrine of justification by faith is established in the first five chapters. Then in the sixth and seventh, though the believer is represented as dead to sin and the law and married to Christ, yet a dreadful struggle goes on in the heart of the regenerate man as long as he has not got the full power of the Holy Spirit. But in the eighth chapter, it is the "law of the Spirit of life in Christ Jesus" that maketh us free from "the law of sin and death." Then we are "not in the flesh, but in the Spirit," with the Spirit of God dwelling in us. All the teaching leads up to the Holy Spirit.

Look also at the Epistle to the Galatians. We always talk of this Epistle as the great source of instruction on the doctrine of justification by faith: but have you ever noticed how the doctrine of the Holy Spirit holds a most prominent place there? Paul asks the

A WORD TO WORKERS

Galatian church: "Received ye the Spirit by the works
of the law, or by the hearing of faith?" It was the
hearing of faith that led them to the full enjoyment of
the Spirit's power. If they sought to be justified by the
works of the law, they had "fallen from grace." "For
we *through the Spirit* wait for the hope of righteousness
by faith." And then at the end of the fifth chapter, we
are told: "If we live in the Spirit, let us walk in the
Spirit."

Again, if we go to the Epistles to the Corinthians,
we find Paul asking the Christians in Corinth: "Know
ye not that your body is the temple of the Holy Ghost
which is in you?" If we look into the Epistle to the
Ephesians, we find the doctrine of the Holy Spirit
mentioned twelve times. It is the Spirit that seals God's
people; "Ye were sealed with that Holy Spirit of
promise." He illumines them; "that God may give the
Spirit of wisdom and revelation in the knowledge of
Him." Through Christ, both Jew and Gentile "have
access by one Spirit unto the Father." They "are
builded together for an habitation of God through the
Spirit." They are "strengthened with might by His
Spirit in the inner man." With "all lowliness and
meekness, with long-suffering, forbearing one another
in love," they are to be "endeavouring to keep the
unity of the Spirit in the bond of peace." We are to
"grieve not the Holy Spirit of God. Paul exhorts
believers to be "filled with the Spirit," "singing and
making melody in your heart to the Lord," thus
glorifying Him. Just study these Epistles carefully, and
you will find that what I say is true—the apostle Paul
takes great pains to lead Christians to the Holy Ghost as
the consummation of the Christian life.

It was the Holy Ghost who was given to the

church at Pentecost; and it is the Holy Ghost who gives
pentecostal blessings now. It is His power, given to
bless men, that wrought such wonderful life, and love,
and self-sacrifice in the early church; and it is this that
makes us look back to those days as the most beautiful
part of the church's history. And it is the same Spirit of
power that must dwell in the hearts of all believers in
our day to give the church its true position. Let us ask
God, then, that every minister and Christian worker
may be endued with the power of the Holy Ghost, that
He may search us, try us, and enable us sincerely to
answer the question, "Have I known the indwelling
and the filling of the Holy Spirit that God wants me to
have?" Let each one of us ask himself: "Is it my great
study to know the Holy Ghost dwelling in me, so that I
may help others to yield to the same indwelling of the
Holy Spirit and that He may reveal Christ fully in His
divine saving and keeping power?" Will not every one
have to confess: "Lord, I have all too little understood
this; I have all too little manifested this in my work and
preaching"? Beloved brethren, "The first duty of every
clergyman is to humbly ask God that all that he wants
done in his hearers may be first fully and truly done in
himself." And the second thing is his duty towards
those who are awakened and brought to Christ—to
lead them on to the full knowledge of the presence and
indwelling of the Holy Spirit.

Now, if we are indeed to come into full harmony
with these two great principles, then there comes to us
some further questions of the very deepest importance.
And the first question is: Why is it that there is in the
church of Christ so little practical acknowledgment of
the power of the Holy Ghost? I am not speaking to
you, brethren, as if I thought you were not sound in

doctrine on this point. I speak to you as believing in the Holy Ghost as the Third Person in the ever-blessed Trinity. But I speak to you confidently, as to those who will readily admit that the truth or the presence of the power of the Holy Ghost is not acknowledged in the church as it ought to be. Then the question is: Why is it not so acknowledged? I answer, because of its spirituality. It is one of the most difficult truths in the Bible for the human mind to comprehend. God has revealed Himself in creation throughout the whole universe. He has revealed Himself in Christ incarnate—and what a subject of study the person, and word, and works of Christ form! But the mysterious indwelling of the Holy Spirit, hidden in the depths of the life of the believer, how much less easy to comprehend!

In the early pentecostal days of the church, this knowledge was intuitive; they *possessed* the Spirit in power. But, soon after, the spirit of the world began to creep into the church and mastered it. This was followed by the deeper darkness of formality and superstition in the Roman Catholic Church, when the spirit of the world completely triumphed in what was improperly styled the church of Christ. The Reformation in the days of Luther restored the truth of justification by faith in Christ; but the doctrine of the Holy Ghost did not then obtain its proper place, for God does not reveal all truth at one time. A great deal of the spirit of the world was still left in the reformed churches; but now God is awakening the church to strive after a fuller scriptural idea of the Holy Spirit's place and power. Through the medium of books, and discussions, and conventions, many hearts are being stirred.

Brethren, it is our privilege to take part in this

great movement; and let us engage in the work more earnestly than ever. Let each of us say that our great work is in preaching Christ—to lead men to the acknowledging of the Holy Spirit, who alone can glorify Christ. I may try to glorify Christ in my preaching, but it will avail nothing without the Spirit of God. I may urge men to the practice of holiness and every Christian virtue, but all my persuasion will avail very little unless I help them to believe that they must have the Holy Ghost dwelling in them, every moment enabling to live the life of Christ. The great reason why the Holy Spirit was given from heaven was to make Christ Jesus' presence manifest to us. While Jesus was incarnate, His disciples were too much under the power of the flesh to allow Christ to get a lodgment in their hearts. It was needful, He said, that He should go away, in order that the Spirit might come; and He promised to those who loved Him and kept His commandments that, with the Spirit, He would come, and the Father would also come, and They would make Their abode with them. It is, thus, the Holy Spirit's great work to reveal the Father and the Son in the hearts of God's people. If we believe and teach men that the Holy Spirit can make Christ a reality to them every moment, men will learn to believe and accept Christ's presence and power, of which they now know far too little.

Then another question presents itself, viz., What are we to expect when the Holy Spirit is duly acknowledged and received? I ask this question, because there is something I have frequently noticed with considerable interest—and, I may say, with some anxiety. I sometimes hear men praying earnestly for a baptism of the Holy Spirit, that He may give them power for their work. Beloved brethren, we need this power, not only for work, but for our daily life. Remember, we must have it all the time. In Old Testament times, the Spirit came with power upon the prophets and other inspired men; but He did not dwell permanently in them.

In the same way, in the church of the Corinthians, the Holy Spirit came with power to work miraculous gifts, and yet they had but a small measure of His sanctifying grace. You will remember the carnal strife, envying, and divisions there were. They had gifts of utterance, gifts of knowledge and wisdom, etc.; but, alas! pride, unlovingness, and other sins sadly marred the character of many of them. And what does this teach us? That a man may have a great gift of power for work, yet very little of the indwelling Spirit. In 1 Corinthians 13, we are reminded that though we may have faith that would remove mountains, if we have not love, we are nothing. We must have the love that brings the humility and self-sacrifice of Jesus. Don't let us put in the first place the gifts we may possess; if we do, we shall have very little blessing. But we should seek, in the first place, that the Spirit of God should come as a light and power of holiness from the indwelling Jesus. Let the first work of the Holy Spirit be to humble you deep down in the very dust, so that your whole life shall be a tender, broken-hearted waiting on God, in the consciousness of mercy coming from above.

Do not seek large gifts; there is something deeper you need. It is not enough that a tree shoots its branches to the sky and is covered thickly with leaves; we want its roots to strike deeply into the soil. Let the thought of the Holy Spirit's being in us—and our hope of being filled with the Spirit—be always accompanied in us with a broken and contrite heart. Let us bow very low before God, in waiting for His grace to fill and to sanctify us. We do not want a power that God might allow us to use, while our inner part is unsanctified. We want God to give us full possession of Himself. In due time, the special gift may come; but we want first and now the power of the Holy Ghost working something far mightier and more effectual in us than any such gift. We should seek, therefore, not only a baptism of power, but a baptism of holiness; we should seek that the inner nature be sanctified by the indwelling of Jesus, and then other power will come as needed.

There is a third question. Suppose someone says to me, "I have given myself up to be filled with the Spirit, and I do not feel that there is any difference in my condition; there is no change of experience that I can speak of. What must I then think? Must not I think that my surrender was not honest?" No, do not think that. "But how then? Does God give no response?" Beloved, God gives a response, but that is not always within certain months or years. "What, then, would you have me do?" Retain the position you have taken before God, and maintain it every day. Say, "O God, I have given myself to be filled; here I am an empty vessel, trusting and expecting to be filled by Thee." Take that position every day and every hour. Ask God to write it across your heart. Give up to God an empty, conse-crated vessel that He may fill it with the Holy Spirit. Take that position constantly. It may be that you are not fully prepared. Ask God to cleanse you, to give you grace to separate from everything sinful—from unbe-lief or whatever hindrance there may be. Then take your position before God and say, "My God, Thou art faithful; I have entered into covenant with Thee for Thy Holy Spirit to fill me, and I believe Thou wilt fulfil it." Brethren, I say for myself, and for every minister of the gospel, and for every fellow-worker, man or woman, that if we thus come before God with a full surrender, in a bold, believing attitude, God's promise must be fulfilled.

If you were to ask me of my own experience, I would say that there have been times when I hardly knew myself what to think of God's answer to my prayer in this matter; but I have found it my joy and my strength to take and maintain my position, and say: "My God, I have given myself up to Thee. It was Thine own grace that led me to Christ; and I stand before Thee in confidence that Thou wilt keep Thy covenant with me to the end. I am the empty vessel; Thou art the God that fillest all." God is faithful, and He gives the promised blessing in His own time and method. Beloved, for God's sake, be content with nothing less than full health and full spiritual life. "Be filled with the Spirit."

Let me return now to the two expressions with which I began: "The first duty of every clergyman is to humbly ask God that all that he wants done in his hearers may be first fully and truly done in himself." Brethren, I ask you, is it not the longing of your hearts to have a congregation of believers filled with the Holy Ghost? Is it not your unceasing prayer for the church of Christ, in which you minister, that the Spirit of holiness, the very Spirit of God's Son, the Spirit of unworldliness and of heavenly-mindedness, may possess it; and that the Spirit of victory and of power over sin may fill its children? If you are willing for that to come, your first duty is to have it yourself.

And then the second sentence: "The first business of a clergyman, when he sees men awakened and brought to Christ, is to lead them on to know the Holy Spirit." How can I do my work with success? I can conceive what a privilege it is to be led by the Spirit of God in all that I am doing; in studying my Bible, praying, visiting, organizing, or whatever I am doing, God is willing to guide me by His Holy Spirit. It sometimes becomes a humiliating experience to me that I am unwatchful and do not wait for the blessing; when that is the case, God can bring me back again. But there is also the blessed experience of God's guiding hand, often through deep darkness, by His Holy Spirit. Let us walk about among the people as men of God, that we may not only preach about a book, and what we believe with our hearts to be true, but may preach what we are and what we have in our own experience. Jesus calls us *witnesses* for Him; what does that mean? The Holy Ghost brought down from heaven to men a participation in the glory and the joy of the exalted Christ. Peter and the others who spoke with Him were filled with this heavenly Spirit; and thus Christ spoke in them and accomplished the work for them. O brethren, if you and I be Christ's, we should take our places and claim our privilege. We are witnesses to the truth that we believe, witnesses to the reality of what Jesus does and what He is by His presence in our own souls. If we are willing to be such witnesses for Christ, let us go to our God; let us make confession and surrender and by faith claim what God has for us as ministers of the gospel and workers in His service. God will prove faithful. Even at this very moment, He will touch our hearts with a deep consciousness of His faithfulness and of His presence; and He will give to every hungering, trustful one that which we continually need.

CONSECRATION

CONSECRATION

But who am I, and what is my people, that we should be able to offer so willingly after this sort? for all things come of thee, and of thine own have we given thee (1 Chron. 29:14).

T O be able to offer anything to God is a perfect mystery. Consecration is a miracle of grace. "All things come of Thee, and of Thine own have we given Thee." In these words there are four very precious thoughts I want to try to make clear to you:

1. God is the owner of all and gives all to us.

2. We have nothing but what we receive, but everything we need we may receive from God.

3. It is our privilege and honor to give back to God what we receive from Him.

4. God has a double joy in His possessions when He receives back from us what He gave.

And when I apply this to my life—to my body, to my wealth, to my property, to my whole being with all its powers—then I understand what consecration ought to be.

IT IS THE GLORY OF GOD —AND HIS VERY NATURE— TO BE ALWAYS GIVING.

God is the owner of all. There is no power, no wealth, no goodness, no love, outside of God. It is the very nature of God, that He does not live for Himself but for His creatures. His is a love that always delights to give. Here we come to the first step in consecration. I must see that everything I have is given by Him; I must learn to believe in God as the great owner and giver of all. Let me hold that fast. I have nothing but what actually and definitely belongs to God. Just as much as people say, "this money in my purse belongs to me," so God is the proprietor of all. It is His and His only. And it is His life and delight to be always giving. Oh, take that precious thought: *There is nothing that God has that He does not want to give.* It is His nature; and, therefore, when God asks anything of you, He must give it first Himself, and He will. Never be afraid whatever God asks; for God only asks what is His own; what He asks you to give He will first Himself give you. The possessor, and owner, and giver of all! This is our God. You can apply this to yourself and your powers to all you are and have. Study it, believe it, live in it, every day, every hour, every moment.

IT IS THE NATURE AND GLORY OF MAN TO BE ALWAYS RECEIVING.

What did God make us for? We have been made to be each of us a vessel into which God can pour out His life, His beauty, His happiness, His love. We are created to be each a receptacle and a reservoir of divine heavenly life and blessing, just as much as God can put into us. Have we understood this, that our great work—the object of our creation—is to be always receiving? If we fully enter into this, it will teach some precious things. One thing is this—the utter folly of being proud or conceited. What an idea! Suppose I were to borrow a very beautiful dress and walk about boasting of it as if it were my own; you might say, "What a fool!" The everlasting God owns everything we have; shall we dare to exalt ourselves on account of what is all His? Then what a blessed lesson it will teach us of what our position is! I have to do with a God whose nature is to be always giving, mine to be always receiving. Just as the lock and key fit each other, God the giver and I the receiver fit into each other. How often we trouble about things—and about praying for them—instead of going back to the root of things, and saying, "Lord, I only crave to be the receptacle of what the will of God means for me, of the power and the gifts and the love and Spirit of God." What can be more simple? Come as a *receptacle*—cleansed, emptied, and humble. Come, and then God will delight to give. If I may with reverence say it, He cannot help Himself; it is His promise, His nature. The blessing is ever flowing out of Him. You know how water always flows into the lowest places. If we would but be emptied and low, nothing but receptacles, what a blessed life we could live! Day by day just praising Him: "Thou givest and I accept. Thou bestowest and I rejoice to receive." How many tens of thousands of people have said this morning: "What a beautiful day! Let us throw open the windows and bring in the sunlight with its warmth and cheerfulness!" May our hearts learn every moment to drink in the light and sunshine of God's love.

"Who am I, and what is my people, that we should be able to offer so willingly after this sort? for all things come of Thee, and we have given Thee of Thine own."

If God gives all and I receive all, then the third thought is very simple:

I MUST GIVE ALL BACK AGAIN.

What a privilege that for the sake of having me in loving, grateful intercourse with Him, and giving me the happiness of pleasing and serving Him, the everlasting God should say, "Come now, and bring Me back all that I give." And yet people say, "Oh, but must I give everything back?" My brother, don't you know that there is no happiness or blessedness except in giving to God! David felt it. He said: "Lord, what an unspeakable privilege it is to be allowed to give that back to Thee that which is Thine own!" Just to receive and then to render back in love to Him, as God, what He gives. Do you know what God needs you for? People say, "Does not God give us all good gifts to enjoy?" But do you know that the reality of the enjoyment is in the giving back? Just look at Jesus; God gave Him a wonderful body. He kept it holy and gave it as a sacrifice to God. This is the beauty of having a body. God has given you a soul; this is the beauty of having a soul—you can give it back to God. People talk about the difficulty they meet with in having so strong a will. You never can have too strong a will, but the trouble is we do not give that strong will up to God, to make it a vessel in which God can and will pour His Spirit, so as to fit it to do splendid service for Himself.

We have now had the three thoughts: God gives all; I receive all; I give up all. Will you do this now? Will not every heart say, "My God, teach me to give up everything"? Take your head, your mind with all its powers of thought, your tongue with all its power of speaking, your property, your heart with its affections—the best and most secret—your gold and silver, everything, and lay it at God's feet and say, "Lord, here is the covenant between me and Thee. Thou delightest to give all, and I delight to give back all." God teach us that. If that simple lesson were learnt, there would be an end of so much trouble about finding out the will of God, and an end of all our holding back, for it would be written, not upon our foreheads, but across our hearts, "God can do with me what He pleases; I belong to Him with all I have." Instead of always saying to God, "Give, give, give," we should say, "Yes, Lord, Thou *dost* give, Thou dost *love* to give, and I love to give back." Try that life, and find out if it is not the very highest life.

God gives all, I receive all, I give all. Now comes the fourth thought:

GOD DOES SO REJOICE IN WHAT WE GIVE TO HIM.

It is not only that I am the receiver and the giver; God is the giver and the receiver too and, may I say it with reverence, has more pleasure in receiving back than even in giving. With our little faith we often think our gifts come back to God all defiled. God says, "No, they come back beautiful and glorified." The surrender of the dear child of His, with his aspirations and thanksgivings, brings them to God with a new value and beauty. Ah! child of God, you do not know how precious the gift that you bring to your Father is in His sight. Have I not seen a mother give a piece of cake, and the child comes and offers her a piece to share it with her? How that mother values the gift! And your God, oh, my friends, your God, His heart, His Father's heart of love, longs, longs, longs to have you give Him everything. It is not a demand. It *is* a demand, but it is not a demand of a hard Master; it is the call of a loving Father, who knows that every gift you bring to God will bind you closer to Himself, and every surrender you make will open your heart wider to get more of His spiritual gifts.

O friends, a gift to God has in His sight infinite value. It delights Him. He sees of the travail of His soul and is satisfied. And it brings unspeakable blessing to you. These are the thoughts our text suggests; now comes the practical application. What are the lessons? We here learn what the true dispositions of the Christian life are.

First, you are to be and abide in continual dependence upon God. Become nothing; begin to understand that you are nothing but an earthen vessel into which God will shine down the treasure of His love. Blessed is the man who knows what it is to be nothing, to be just an empty vessel meet for God's use. Work, the apostle says, for it is God who worketh in you to will and to do. Brethren, come now and take the place of deep, deep dependence on God. And then take the place of *childlike trust* and expectancy. Count upon your God to do for you everything that you can desire of Him. Honor God as a God who gives liberally. Honor God and believe that He asks nothing from you but what He is going first to give. And then come praise and surrender and consecration. Praise Him for it! Let every sacrifice to Him be a thank-offering. What are we going to consecrate? First of all our lives. There are perhaps men and women—young men and women—whose hearts are asking, "What do you want me to do—to say I will be a missionary?" No, indeed, I do not ask you to do this. Deal with God, and come to Him and say, "Lord of all, I belong to Thee, I am absolutely at Thy disposal." Yield up yourselves. There may be many who cannot go as missionaries, but oh, come, give up yourselves to God all the same to be consecrated to the work of His kingdom. Let us bow down before Him. Let us give Him all our powers—our head to think for His kingdom, our heart to go out in love for men—and however feeble you may be, come and say: "Lord, here I am, to live and die for Thy kingdom."

Some talk and pray about the filling of the Holy Spirit. Let them pray more and believe more. But remember the Holy Spirit came to fit men to be messengers of the kingdom, and you cannot expect to be filled with the Spirit unless you want to live for Christ's kingdom. You cannot expect all the love and peace and joy of heaven to come into your life and be your treasures, unless you give them up absolutely to the kingdom of God and possess and use them only for Him. It is the soul utterly given up to God that will receive in its emptying the fullness of the Holy Spirit. Dear friends, we must consecrate not only ourselves—body and soul—but all we have.

Some of you may have children; perhaps you have an only child, and you dread the very idea of letting it go. Take care, take care; God deserves your confidence, your love, and your surrender. I plead with you; take your children and say to Jesus: "Anything, Lord, that pleases Thee." Educate your children for Jesus. God helps you to do it. He may not accept all of them for Christian work, but He will accept your willingness, and there will be a rich blessing in your soul for it.

Then there is money. When I hear appeals for money from every society; when I hear calculations as to what the Christians of England are spending on pleasure and the small amount given for missions, I say there is something terrible in it. God's children with so much wealth and comfort, giving away so small a portion! God be praised for every exception! But there are many who give but very little, who never so give that it costs them something, and they feel it. Oh, friends! our giving must be in proportion to God's giving. He gives you all. Let us take it up in our consecration prayer: "Lord, take it all, every penny I possess. It is all Thine." Let us often say, "It is all His." You may not know how much you ought to give. Give up all, put everything in His hands, and He will teach you if you will wait.

We have heard this precious message from David's mouth. We Christians of the nineteenth century, have we learned to know our God, who is willing to give everything? God help us to.

And then the second message. We have nothing that we do not receive, and we may receive everything if we are willing to stand before God and take it.

Thirdly, whatever you have received from God, give it back. It brings a double blessing to your own soul.

Fourthly, whatever God receives back from us comes to Him in heaven and gives Him infinite joy and happiness, as He sees His object has been attained. Let us come in the spirit of David, with the spirit of Jesus Christ in us. Let us pray our consecration prayer. And may the blessed Spirit give each of us grace to think and to say the right thing, and to do what shall be pleasing in the Father's sight.